CALDER

MOBILIST / RINGMASTER / INNOVATOR

BY DAVID BOURDON

MACMILLAN PUBLISHING CO., INC., New York
COLLIER MACMILLAN PUBLISHERS, London

PHOTOGRAPHIC CREDITS

Pages 100, 110–11, 124, David Bourdon; 126–127, courtesy
Braniff International; 7 courtesy City Archives of
Philadelphia; 123, William T. Conroy, Jr.; 5 (right), 31, 43,
78, 79, 99, 108, 109, 112, 114, 120, Pedro E. Guerrero;
10 (C.P. Shoemaker), 11, 12, 13, 16 (right), 17, 25 (left),
courtesy Margaret Calder Hayes; 117, courtesy Mary Ann Keeler;
122, Les Levine; 121, Fred W. McDarrah; 30, 42, 54, 73, 76,
80, 82, Herbert Matter; 55, Herbert K. Nolan; 2, 4, 39, 63,
71, 81, 84, 85, 88, 91, 96, 128, courtesy Perls Galleries; ii, 1,
97, 105, 134, Harry Shunk.

June 1980

Copyright © 1980 David Bourdon
Copyright © 1980 Macmillan Publishing Co., Inc.

All rights reserved. No part of this book may be reproduced
or transmitted in any form or by any means, electronic or
mechanical, including photocopying, recording or by any
information storage and retrieval system, without
permission in writing from the Publisher.

Macmillan Publishing Co., Inc.
866 Third Avenue, New York, NY. 10022
Collier Macmillan Canada, Ltd.

Printed in the United States of America

10   9   8   7   6   5   4   3   2   1

LIBRARY OF CONGRESS CATALOGING IN PUBLICATION DATA
Bourdon, David.
    Calder: mobilist, ringmaster, innovator.

    Bibliography: p.
    Includes index.
    SUMMARY: Presents the life and representative
works of artist Alexander Calder
against the world of contemporary art.
    1. Calder, Alexander, 1898-1976.
2. Sculptors—United States—Biography.
[1. Calder, Alexander, 1898-1976. 2. Sculptors]
I. Title.
NB237.C28B68   709'.2'4 [B] [92]   72-92447
ISBN 0-02-711780-4

CONTENTS

ACKNOWLEDGMENTS

BY THE TIME I MET ALEXANDER CALDER in 1975 he had been widely acclaimed as an important artist for almost half a century. Even at his advanced age he was still prolific, turning out a prodigious number of giant stabiles, mobiles and various editions of original prints, posters and textiles. While endeavoring to concentrate all his energies on his work, he was also under tremendous pressure to devote some of his time to tasks that he often found bothersome—attending committee meetings about commissions for large works, assembling information for museum exhibitions and catalogs, and granting interviews to the press. Impatient to get on with his work, he did not relish spending valuable time discussing the past. Consequently, I was unable to ask him many questions that continue to intrigue me.

Fortunately, there is an abundance of published material available on Calder. Since he was among the most newsworthy of artists, much of his life and art is chronicled in newspapers and magazines, not to mention numerous books. I should like to cite here a few of the many books and exhibition catalogs that proved particularly helpful to me in my research.

The one book that is "must" reading for any Calder fan is, obviously, the artist's autobiography, a chatty, spirited account of an eventful life, told with gusto and good humor. A second primary source that the artist's admirers will certainly want to consult is the delightful family memoir written by "Sandy" Calder's sister, "Peggy"—Margaret Calder Hayes. Mrs. Hayes's book provides an enchanting account of her and Sandy's childhood and vividly portrays the lively personalities of their parents and grandparents. The two books by Sandy and Peggy complement each other and together constitute an incomparable introduction to an extraordinary artist and his fascinating family. I also wish to thank Mrs. Hayes for permitting me to republish some of her wonderful family photographs. Her generosity in sharing information about the Calder family is greatly appreciated.

Among the art writers who have made the meaning and achievement of Calder's work more visible, I particularly admire James Johnson Sweeney, one of the first to recognize Calder's importance. Sweeney's early writings on Calder are still among the best. I also learned a great deal from H. H. Arnason and Bernice Rose, whose texts on Calder are models of discerning scholarship and critical scrutiny. For an entertaining blend of information and warm appreciation, one need look no further than the writings of Jean Lipman, a long-time friend of Calder and one of his most ardent collectors.

Additional details about all of the above books and catalogs are provided in the bibliography.

Much of the pertinent information about Calder is in pictorial form, taken by photographers whose documentary images grow in importance with the years. I consider myself fortunate to include in this book photographs by such gifted photographers as Herbert Matter, who began photographing Calder in the late 1930s, and Pedro E. Guerrero and Harry Shunk, whose memorable portraits of the artist date from the 1960s.

Among Calder's dealers, I am particularly grateful to Klaus G. Perls, the artist's New York dealer for more than two decades. Mr. Perls provided encouragement and help at every stage of the project, establishing contacts and supplying information and photographs. At New York's Willard Gallery, where Calder exhibited in the early 1940s, Dan Johnson graciously permitted me to examine gallery records. I also was able to check pertinent documents—thanks to a courteous staff—at the Pierre Matisse Gallery (also in New York), where Calder exhibited frequently in the 1930s.

It would be difficult to overpraise the scholarly resources and efficient staffs of the following institutions, which provided me with much of my research material and many of the photographs used in this book: The Archives of American Art, Washington, D.C. and New York; The Solomon R. Guggenheim Museum, New York; The Hirshhorn Museum and Sculpture Garden, Washington, D.C.; The Museum of Modern Art, New York; The National Gallery of Art, Washington, D.C.; The New York Public Library; The Phillips Collection, Washington, D.C.; and The Whitney Museum of American Art, New York.

Finally, I would like to thank a group of people, many of them long-time friends, who offered useful advice and moral support and in one way or another had an impact on the outcome of this book: Alexandra Anderson, Gregory Battcock, Teeny Duchamp, Les Levine, the late Lida Livingston, Joan M. Marter, Barnett Owen, Michael Richman, John Russell, Dorothy Seiberling and Edmund White.

CALDER

EARLY ONE MORNING IN THE SUMMER OF 1922, Alexander Calder awoke on the deck of a ship off the coast of Guatemala. He had fallen asleep on a makeshift couch—a coil of heavy rope. The sea was calm but as the young man peered out toward the horizon, he saw a startling sight. What looked like a fiery red blob, enormous and pulsating, rose slowly out of the sea. It took him a moment to realize that the blazing object was the rising sun. Off in the opposite direction, where the sky was still dark, he observed the moon, shiny as a silver coin, gliding gracefully across the horizon. Of all the things that the twenty-three-year-old Calder was to see on the voyage, that sun and moon, performing a sort of aerial ballet, impressed him most. It left him with a lasting sensation of the stark beauty and astonishing mechanics of the solar system.

Several years later, when Calder was thirty-five and had abandoned his brief career as a sailor, he invented a new type of sculpture, partly inspired by that vision of the sun and moon. Using bits and pieces of sheet metal and wire, he constructed works of art in which various elements revolved around one another like planetary bodies in the solar system. His realization that some parts could be at rest while others moved in eccentric patterns struck him, he said, as "the ideal source of form." Because Calder's

1

Calder

constructions are capable of movement, they became known as "mobiles."

Mobiles.

For thousands of years, most sculpture had been carved out of a mass of rock or marble. Sculpture was almost always a solid, freestanding, three-dimensional object. It might represent an active human figure, but the sculpture itself remained static.

Unlike traditional sculpture, Calder's mobiles generally hang from the ceiling and have no solid core. Moreover, the rhythmic movements that the mobiles go through are just as important to the overall composition as the shapes of the metal blades and wire rods.

During his long and amazingly productive career, Calder created thousands of artworks. In addition to mobiles, he produced scores of non-moving sculptures, which he called "stabiles." Several of these are more than fifty feet high. He made countless drawings, gouaches and lithographs, and he designed jewelry, stage settings and tapestries. Although he created impressive works in all these fields, it is the mobiles that sent his reputation as one of the most original sculptors of the twentieth century into orbit.

Arctic Sunset, c. 1973. Gouache, 29¼" x 43". Perls Galleries, New York.

While most mobiles hang from the ceiling, Calder also constructed a great many mobiles that project from the wall, or balance atop a standing base on the floor. A typical mobile consists of several flat pieces of metal, cut into rounded or angular shapes and fastened to lengths of wire, which are looped to one another so that each is capable of spinning independently. Like sails, the flat pieces of metal are set in motion by any passing breeze. A touch of the hand or the slightest whiff of air is enough to activate a mobile, causing the various elements to whirl and glide through space, and recompose themselves in ever-changing arrangements.

Calder's mobiles are usually abstract; that is, they are not intended to be literal representations of anything in nature. Yet many of their shapes and movements look as if they were inspired by various animals or plants. Certain mobiles make people think of a flock of birds circling about in the sky, butterflies flitting capriciously through the air, or big lily pads swaying slightly as they float on the water.

As soon as he finished a sculpture, Calder named it after whatever came to mind. For instance, in 1948 he made a hanging mobile with three clusters of wire "branches," each with a series of white disks in graduated sizes. Because it reminded him of snowflakes fluttering about in a draft, he named it "Snow Flurry I" (*opposite, left*). One of his standing mobiles, made in 1974, resembles a trained seal performing a complicated juggling act. This whimsical creature stands on two flippers and a long tail bent into

Very Crinkly, c. 1974. Standing mobile: painted sheet metal, wire, 10" x 18". Collection Mr. and Mrs. Bernhard S. Blumenthal, Philadelphia.

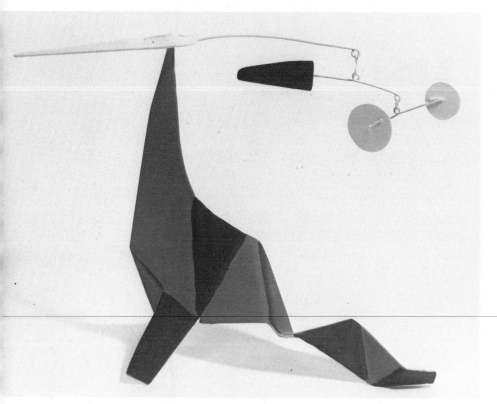

geometric sections; its upraised nose balances a long wire from which dangle a set of leaflike blades. Because of the many angular bends in its tail, it was given an appropriate name: "Very Crinkly" (*left*).

Many mobiles behave as if they have personalities of their own. Some move sluggishly, like big, ponderous animals, so lethargic in their movements that they could be imitating hippopotamuses lolling about in a mud bath. Others move with the brisk precision of an agitated bird, hopping from branch to branch. Some mobiles move with calm grace, while others are jittery and giddy.

Calder was a big, burly bear of a man who in his later years had tousled white hair, silvery eyebrows and an intense pink complexion. Because he usually wore a red-flannel shirt and khaki pants, he looked like a jolly combination of

OPPOSITE LEFT: *Snow Flurry I*, 1948. Hanging mobile: painted sheet steel and steel wire, 7'10" x 70¼". The Museum of Modern Art, New York; gift of the artist.
OPPOSITE RIGHT: Alexander Calder concentrated utmost attention on every aspect of his mobiles, from the precise balancing of the cut-metal "leaves" to the carefully chosen colors in which he painted them. His mobiles refer to a wide variety of natural phenomena, ranging from delicately swirling snowflakes to the whimsical antics of imaginary, long-tailed animals.

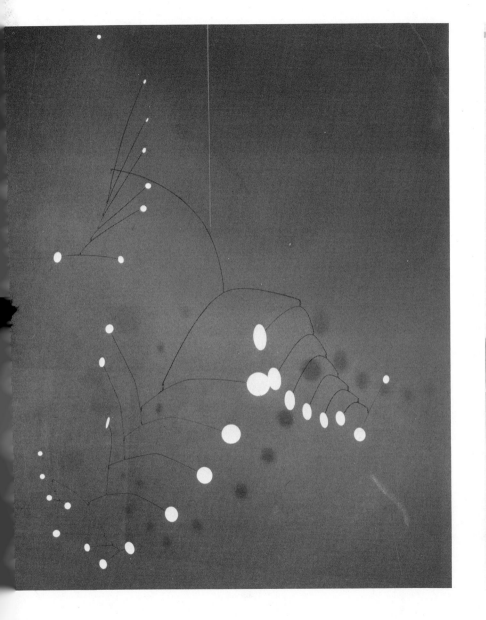

Santa Claus and a baggy-pants clown. Everyone called him Sandy.

He stood with an uncertain posture, like a child just learning how to walk. When he spoke, it was in grunts and mumbles. It was said that only two kinds of people ever listened to Sandy: those who could not understand a single word and those who thought they did.

He disliked talking about art, either his own or that of others. He might explain how a particular piece was made, but he never elaborated upon its "meaning"—its philosophical or artistic significance.

Calder was the only American sculptor of his generation to become an artist of international stature. During the twenties and thirties, it was especially difficult for any American artist to be a "modernist." To be a modernist means that one deliberately breaks with the traditions of the past, and consciously seeks new forms of expression. Because the United States was artistically backward at the time, most ambitious artists of Sandy's generation went to Paris to study art. The French capital was also the center of the art world. But most American artists who gathered there turned out work that was only a pale reflection of the current styles being practiced in Paris.

Calder went to Paris and managed to make a new type of art that even the sophisticated Parisians thought was modern. In Paris he was fortunate to experience at firsthand a great deal of the most innovative art being produced there. He was not always able to recognize what art was really new and important. While trying to find his own way, he sometimes borrowed from other artists. He might borrow an idea from this artist and a particular form from that artist, but then he would put it all together in a way that was entirely his own.

The kind of artistic background that Sandy had to overcome is best illustrated by his own family. He was brought up by parents who made art of a very different kind—not nearly so original. Both his father and mother were conscientious, gifted artists. But while they were extremely accomplished by traditional American standards, they did not contribute many significant new ideas or forms.

It is ironic that Calder, who never seemed to have any clearcut ambitions or goals, should emerge as one of the most important pioneers of American modernism. As a young man he was quiet, easily distracted and not particularly promising, and it is still a little surprising that he amounted to anything at all. Sandy really stumbled into the mainstream of modern art by accident. But, however he entered the mainstream, he made quite a splash.

CALDER WAS BORN IN LAWNTON, a suburb of Philadelphia, on July 22, 1898. He was named Alexander after his father, Alexander Stirling Calder, and his grandfather, Alexander Milne Calder. The youngest Alexander, who was nicknamed Sandy to help distinguish him from the other two, grew up in a family in which being an artist was almost a tradition. His father and grandfather were both sculptors who attained considerable success by the standards of their time. His mother was a painter. Although Sandy grew up surrounded by art, he did not develop much interest in it until he was nearly twenty-five.

Grandfather Calder reached the pinnacle of his career—the top of Philadelphia's City Hall—in the early 1890s. Alexander Milne Calder, who was born in Aberdeen, Scotland, in 1846, studied sculpture in Edinburgh. After three years of study, he traveled to London and Paris and then emigrated in 1868, at age twenty-two, to the United States, where he settled in Philadelphia. During the next few years he studied at the Pennsylvania Academy of the Fine Arts, modeled sculpture and architectural decorations for a number of Philadelphia architects, married Margaret Stirling and became a United States citizen.

Only four years after his arrival in the United States, Calder received a stroke of good luck when he was hired to design and model groups of figures for Philadelphia's new City Hall. Today, he is known chiefly for his thirty-seven-foot-high bronze statue of William Penn (*below*), which still stands on top of Philadelphia's City Hall. The project, which took about twenty years to complete, presents Penn—the English Quaker who founded the city—as a heroic-looking young man, wearing a wide-brimmed hat, a long jacket

2

Alexander Milne Calder, *William Penn*, 1894. Bronze, 37' h. Philadelphia City Hall, Philadelphia.

and a sober expression. In physical size, Penn is imposing. His nose is thirteen inches long and the buttons on his coat are six inches in diameter. The 60,000-pound statue is so huge that it had to be taken apart and hoisted in thirteen sections to the top of the City Hall tower, where it has stood since 1894.

Calder had six sons, the most successful being Alexander Stirling, who was born in Philadelphia in 1870. As a youth, Stirling was not particularly interested in art—an attitude that later would also be demonstrated by his son Sandy. Stirling was slim and handsome, with an aristocratic profile. He displayed a keen interest in the theater and, starting at the age of sixteen, became an avid theatergoer, seeing all the great actors of his day. In his later years, he claimed that his shyness had inhibited him from becoming an actor himself.

In 1886, Stirling entered the Pennsylvania Academy of the Fine Arts, where he studied drawing under Thomas Eakins, one of the major American artists of the time. After learning to draw from plaster casts of antique sculpture, Stirling was allowed to enter the life class, where he could draw from nude models. Toward the end of his school days, he became a sort of deputy demonstrator of anatomy, with sometimes unpleasant duties in the dissection room. According to Stirling, the "supreme benefit" of attending the Pennsylvania Academy was that he was able to meet there his future wife, Nanette Lederer, a Milwaukee woman three and a half years older than he.

Stirling pursued, with even more zeal than his father, a career in public statuary. He specialized in robust, muscular gods, goddesses, Indians and allegorical figures. He believed that public statuary was the highest goal to which a sculptor could aspire. During his long career, he provided sculptural decorations for many buildings, parks and private gardens all over the country. Two of his most prestigious commissions were for monumental statues of Leif Ericsson in Reykjavik, Iceland, and George Washington as first president, on the western pier of Washington Arch in Manhattan's Washington Square.

Stirling was an idealist who believed passionately in the spiritually uplifting, ennobling qualities of art. He protested some people's tendency to regard sculpture as merely ornamental—and useless. Sculpture, for Stirling, was "supremely useful," as important "as the bread you eat. . . . It has gladdened, inspired, expanded, and enriched the world. Without it, we should not exist."

Stirling maintained that "a work of art cannot be explained in words. If it could, it would not be worth doing as art. That is why we have art, to give us something that words cannot give." He

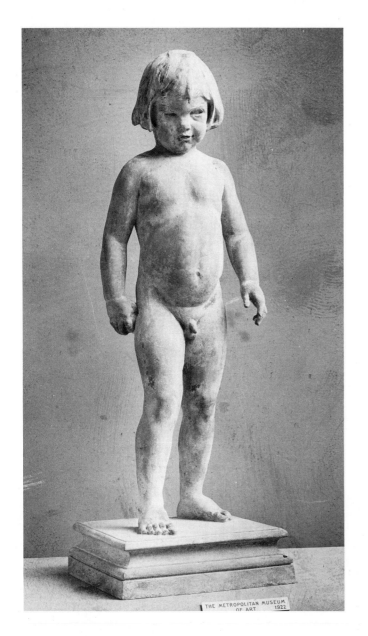

THE METROPOLITAN MUSEUM OF ART 1922

also believed that sculpture attained its highest fulfillment as monumental outdoor art, where it could reach as large a public as possible. ("Indoor sculpture will take care of itself," he snapped.)

Stirling was a more sophisticated sculptor than his father, who pursued a plodding sort of realism. Stirling's style was more graceful and even fanciful, though the figures he sculpted were sometimes marred by excessive sentimentality. However, both artists merit a place in any history of American sculpture.

It was left to Sandy to give the family name an international reputation.

Sandy was his parents' second and last child. His sister Peggy was born two years earlier in Paris, where Stirling and Nanette had gone for an extended stay. When Sandy was three years old, his parents moved from their house in Lawnton to a Philadelphia apartment.

As a child, Sandy was frequently called upon to model for his parents—a tiresome task that bored him. When he was four years old, he spent many hours posing naked, with an orange in one hand, in his father's studio over an old livery stable. The result was one of Stirling's most appealing sculptures, "The Man Cub" (*left*). The

A. Stirling Calder, *The Man Cub,* c. 1902. Bronze, 44" h. The Metropolitan Museum of Art, New York; Rogers Fund, 1922.

9

statue shows Sandy as a pudgy-looking child with one foot hesitantly placed in front of the other. It's a tentative, unbalanced stance that Sandy retained all his life. He also posed for several portraits by his mother. Before long, he learned to turn the situation to his advantage by demanding hourly modeling rates.

Stirling, despite his vigorous appearance, suffered from tuberculosis which prompted him to

LEFT: Sandy was the model for all three boys in this illustration painted in about 1905 by Charlotte Harding, a friend of Nanette Calder, for a children's book, *Dream Blocks.*
ABOVE: Sandy and Peggy in Philadelphia, 1905.

move to the Southwest, with its more healthful climate. In 1905 he and Nanette left the children with friends in Philadelphia and took the train to

Arizona. The following spring, Nanette returned East to collect the children.

Sandy found the train trip long and arduous, but he liked to stand on the observation platform, listening to the noise of the wheels. They finally arrived in Tucson late one evening. The following day, the Calders rode in a stagecoach, drawn by six horses, to Oracle, a small town about forty-five miles away. Arizona—not yet a state, and not admitted to the Union until 1912—was still frontier country, and the ride over dusty roads took all day. The terrain was dry and mountainous, with few signs of civilization amid the seemingly endless expanse of scrub and sagebrush.

Their destination was a "health ranch," a real ranch with cattle that doubled as a sanitarium, mostly for people afflicted with respiratory ailments. Some boarders who stayed there were so eager to fill their lungs with fresh air that they slept outdoors in tents. Sandy and Peggy thought Oracle offered far more adventures and fun than Philadelphia. They saw cactuses, Apaches and mule trains, and they even had their own donkey to ride. In addition, Stirling gave them a small black dog, which he called Kohinoor. The children called him Kohie. There was a cattle roundup in the fall, and Sandy was impressed by the way the cowboys branded the calves. A year or so later, after leaving Oracle,

when he was given some toy horses made out of cowhide stuffed with sawdust, he decided to imitate the cowboys. He fashioned a branding iron out of a piece of wire that had held a roll of toilet paper, heated it, and branded the horses—only to see all the sawdust run out!

Sandy and Peggy cried when it came time to leave Oracle, because Stirling insisted they

Kohinoor, a dog named after a famous Indian diamond, and a burro named Jack-O became the first pets for Sandy and Peggy. Oracle, Arizona, c. 1906.

Stirling and Nanette Calder with their children Sandy and Peggy. Pasadena, California, 1906.

abandon Kohinoor. In the fall of 1906, the Calder family moved west to Los Angeles, a booming town with a population of well over 200,000. There were few automobiles in Los Angeles and many of the streets were still unpaved. But the city had an excellent public transportation system, with electric trolleys that traversed the entire metropolitan area.

The Calders settled in the suburb of Pasadena, moving into a two-story bungalow on a corner lot with plenty of bright geraniums in the front yard. Stirling converted a nearby barn into a studio with a skylight. In addition, he rented another work space in downtown Los Angeles.

In Pasadena, Sandy began to show his mechanical bent and manual dexterity. He was spurred on by Peggy, who gave him a pair of pliers for Christmas. Eventually, he was given other tools and allowed to use the cellar of the house as a workshop. One of the things he most enjoyed making was a miniature castle for Peggy's doll, which was named Thomasine. He constructed the castle in the backyard and excavated a moat around it. Then, having found some copper wire in the street, he devised fanciful jewelry for Thomasine. (As an adult, Calder fashioned a considerable amount of original jewelry from simple materials.) In his easygoing manner, Sandy made all sorts of odds and ends that impressed his schoolmates and the neighboring kids. "My workshop became some sort of a center of attraction," he recalled years later; "everybody came in."

On New Year's Day, 1907, Sandy attended

the Pasadena Tournament of Roses. At that time, the annual parade of floral floats was followed not by a football game, as it is today, but by a four-horse-chariot tournament. Sandy was impressed by the thundering chariot races, but he also enjoyed some of the lesser events, with lighter chariots pulled by four donkeys. They prompted him to construct small chariots for neighborhood races.

Inspired by the stories of King Arthur, Sandy made himself a helmet out of a piece of galvanized iron, using a piece of wire screen to cover the face. He also took a pair of gloves that his mother had given him and converted them into gauntlets by covering them with wire rings and metal. As soon as he was all decked out in his handmade armor, he engaged in mock battle with the son of one of his father's colleagues. Sandy's opponent outflanked him and gave him a good smack on the bottom with the flat blade of the sword. That blow squelched Sandy's interest in chivalry.

Sandy was not athletic and remained indifferent to most sports. A family friend, Arthur Jerome Eddy, who was a prominent lawyer and art collector, offered to pay for a gymnasium course —providing Sandy wanted to take it. To please his parents, Sandy accepted the gift and dutifully attended the gymnasium, where he suffered through the exercises. The next year, Eddy of-

fered Sandy either a bicycle or another physical-fitness course. Sandy chose the bicycle.

Stirling, having regained his health, decided to return east to New York, which he called the "metropolis of art." But instead of heading for New York City, the Calders settled, about 1910, into a small house on a walled estate in Croton-on-Hudson, New York. Stirling took over the large garage on the estate and converted it into a studio with a skylight. Sandy again was given the cellar to use as a workshop.

When he was about nine years old, Sandy designed a toy cannon to shoot ladyfinger firecrackers. The barrel is an empty .22-caliber cartridge. Collection Margaret Calder Hayes, Berkeley, California.

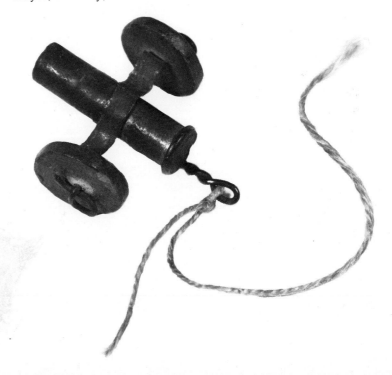

Still in chronic need of fresh air, Stirling installed a bed on the roof of the house, rigging his mattress on a few beams of wood and adding an overhead canvas for protection against the elements. To reach his perch, he had to crawl out Sandy's window each evening.

Although Croton-on-Hudson was only an hour or so north by train from New York City, Stirling felt he needed a studio in the city itself, so that he and his work would be more available to potential clients. He finally rented space in the Tenth Street Studios, a downtown Manhattan building that once had been a hub of the New York art world. Sandy thought the studio was a terrible space and did not understand how his father could work there. According to Sandy, the skylight bleached the top of everything and left vertical surfaces in shadow. But Stirling seemed content with the studio and decided to live closer to it, so he moved his family to a town called Spuyten Duyvil. Sandy began attending Yonkers High School. Once more, he took the cellar as his workshop, still producing toys and household gadgets.

Meanwhile, momentous things were developing in the American art world. A group of New York artists was busily organizing a comprehensive exhibition of modern art that would become one of the pivotal events in American art history —the 1913 Armory Show. The show was officially titled the International Exhibition of Modern Art, and it opened at the Sixty-ninth-Regiment Armory in downtown Manhattan in February 1913. The show had been two years in the making. Its organizers had scoured the studios and galleries of Europe, carefully selecting important examples of modern painting and sculpture. When finally assembled, the exhibition contained more than 1,200 works, including many by American artists.

The Armory Show was thronged with spectators who had never been exposed to modern art before. Most of the public, and even many art lovers, were accustomed to art that realistically represented nature or everyday life. The Armory Show confronted them with a baffling series of isms—Impressionism, Post-Impressionism, Cubism. It looked to some as if all the artists had taken leave of their senses, rendering their subjects with distorted forms and nonnatural colors.

The show created an enormous stir, partly because it had received a great deal of advance publicity, but also because the majority of newspapers and magazines treated it as a moral outrage that could not be sufficiently condemned. Naturally, the curious public flocked to the exhibition to see for themselves whether the paintings and sculpture were as dreadful, disgusting and scandalous as the press reported. Several people accused the show of subverting American art with "mad," "degenerate" new tendencies from Europe; and some critics, who feared the new art would trigger a social, as well as aesthetic, revolution, insistently compared the artists to anarchists and bomb throwers.

The most controversial section of the show—which became known as the "chamber of horrors"—was devoted to Cubist art, the most innovative style in Paris. Here, the star attraction was a painting titled "Nude Descending a Staircase," painted the previous year by a twenty-four-year-old French artist, Marcel Duchamp. Wanting to convey the impression of a moving figure, Duchamp portrayed several overlapping images of a nude woman, superimposed in the manner of a stroboscopic or multiple-exposure photograph. There was constantly a crowd in front of this picture. To many people it appeared completely senseless, since hardly anyone could puzzle out the nude figure. One writer complained it looked more like "an explosion in a shingle factory." The painting assured Duchamp's notoriety in the United States and, when he paid his first visit to New York a couple of years later, he was greeted as a celebrity. Eventually, Duchamp became an influential mentor for many American artists—including Calder, who met him nearly twenty years after the Armory Show.

As a cultural event, the Armory Show was a watershed, separating what was new and modern from the old-fashioned and academic. The show was divisive in several ways. First, it made the American artists look tame in comparison with the Europeans; in fact, it proved conclusively that most American artists were behind the times by European standards. Secondly, the exhibition encouraged people to take sides, converting some artists to modernism, while confirming others as conservative.

Stirling expressed total indifference; he did not participate in, or even bother to attend, the Armory Show. However, he had a good excuse for ignoring the whole thing: in 1912, he was appointed acting chief of sculpture for the Panama-Pacific International Exposition, to take place in San Francisco in 1915. This fair, which celebrated the completion of the Panama Canal, finished in 1914, was to mark the high point of Stirling's career. By the time of the Armory Show opening, he had moved his family back to California and was hard at work on his grandiose designs for the exposition.

The Panama-Pacific International Exposition was notable for the quantity and exuberance of its sculpture. More than 40 sculptors had been invited to contribute designs for scores of sculptures; and Stirling, who had about 160 workers under his supervision, was ultimately responsible for the production and installation of the works. Stirling collaborated with other artists on two large sculptural extravaganzas, "Nations of the East" and "Nations of the West," which called for dozens of human figures. But his most important work, which he designed in its entirety, was the spectacular "Fountain of Energy" (*right*), which occupied the place of honor just inside the main entrance. This colossal fountain helped set the jubilant tone for the entire exposition. The Panama Canal, that triumph of American engineering, could not have received a more grandiloquent tribute than Stirling's fountain.

A. Stirling Calder, *The Fountain of Energy,* Panama-Pacific International Exposition, San Francisco, c. 1915.
The man on horseback symbolizes "energy" in this extravagant tribute to the recently completed Panama Canal. The allegorical figures, reveling in the pool, represent the "great oceans" and "lesser waters."

A. Stirling Calder, *The Stars,* a detail of The Colonnade of Stars, Panama-Pacific International Exposition, San Francisco, c. 1915.

Stirling's second major contribution to the fair was a group of female statues called "The Stars" (*left*). The "Stars" were widely reproduced as the insignia of the fair, and also appeared on the gold and silver badges worn by the various officials.

Sandy, now fifteen, enjoyed living in San Francisco, where he was enrolled at Lowell High School near Golden Gate Park. Once again, he established a cellar workshop in his parents' house. On occasion, he visited his father's enormous workshop on the fair grounds. Sandy seemed largely indifferent to sculpture of any kind, so it apparently never crossed his mind that a work of art could be modern or traditional. Aesthetic issues were entirely over his head at this time. What *did* capture his attention in Stirling's workshop was the pointing machine, a mechanical device used by sculptors to transfer the

A. Stirling Calder, *The Little Mermaid of Viscaya,* c. 1917. The Island, Viscaya, James Deering Estate, Miami, Florida.

measurements of a small-scale model onto larger blocks of stone or marble. The pointing machine had two parallel needles, one longer than the other, that traced the contours of the sculpture. "The small sculpture and the framework for the large sculpture were placed on two turntables which turned together," Sandy recalled years later. "The sculptor would put a cross on the small plaster figure and drive a nail into the wood framework where the other needle came. Rotating all about the high and the low spots, these would be represented by nailheads in the enlarged structure. The gaps between nails would be filled in according to the taste of the sculptor at work. I'd be particularly fascinated by the mechanics, the rotating motions and the parallel needles of the process." It is significant that Sandy, even at this early age, was attracted to a mechanical apparatus that in certain ways forecast his later invention of the mobile, in which the movement of one element generated movement in another.

In the winter of 1914–15, the Calder family moved across the San Francisco Bay to Berkeley. Stirling went to work on a sculptural commission for the Oakland City Hall; Peggy attended the University of California at Berkeley; and Sandy continued his studies at Lowell High School in San Francisco. Peggy joined a sorority and began dating a fellow student, Kenneth Hayes, whom she later married.

Sandy still could not decide what kind of career to pursue. One of his high-school friends announced that he was going to become a mechanical engineer, and Sandy thought that sounded impressive. "I was not very sure what this term meant," he said, "but I thought I'd better adopt it." Stirling consulted the chief engineer at the fair for the name of a good school in the East, and the engineer recommended Stevens Institute of Technology in Hoboken, New Jersey. Stevens, which had opened in 1871, was the first educational institution in the United States to offer a degree in mechanical engineering.

In 1915, the Calder family returned East and settled in New York City. Peggy enrolled for her junior year at Barnard College, and Sandy crossed the river to Hoboken, just west from Manhattan, to learn mechanical engineering.

DURING HIS FRESHMAN YEAR at Stevens Institute of Technology, Calder lived on campus in a building called Castle Stevens. He shared a third-floor room in a square tower overlooking the Hudson River. Although the room had plenty of light and a pleasant view of the river, Calder moved the following year to another room, in order to be with three schoolmates with whom he had become friendly. His easygoing disposition and his tendency to clown around made him popular with his fellow students. He joined the Delta Tau Delta fraternity where most of the other members were athletes, or the sons of prosperous businessmen. While Calder did not fit into either of these categories, he was so affable that he was constantly amusing his fraternity brothers.

Calder excelled in geometry and frequently won perfect scores in his math exams. But he was a poor athlete. The football coach told him: "Anybody who can walk is an athlete."

"I believed him," Calder said, "and tried to play football all the time I was in college, without actually getting into a single game."

In the summer of 1916, Calder spent five weeks learning to be a soldier at the Plattsburg Civilian Military Training Camp in upstate New York. Since 1914, a great war had been spreading across Europe, and it became increasingly evident that the United States was going to be forced to join the conflict. The United States finally declared war on Germany in April 1917, and, the following month, began drafting men between the ages of twenty-one and thirty.

Calder was too young to be drafted. But Stevens Institute made military training compulsory for all students. Because Calder had had some military experience the previous summer, he was made "guide" of his battalion and had to march out in front. This position drew attention to him and, since he had a peculiar way of marching—thrusting his chest and belly forward while arching his back—he was teased as "the man of 400 degrees." During his military training, Calder claimed, "I learned to talk out of the side of my mouth and have never been quite able to correct it since."

Calder and his buddies were happy to learn that they had access to all the military canteens. They proceeded to devote their time to planning their weekends so they could visit their favorite canteen in Brooklyn, "where there were charming girls to dance with." Calder, who claimed to have "perfected" his dancing during this period, was almost disappointed when the war ended in November 1918, forcing the corps of dancing cadets to devote more energy to their studies. Still, there were plenty of dances at school, and even after Calder graduated he would say, "My idea of a pleasant evening was to go to a Stevens dance at my fraternity."

Calder graduated with a degree in mechanical engineering in 1919, then squandered the next three years working at miscellaneous odd jobs. "It was a race between being bounced and quitting," he observed. He worked briefly for an automotive engineer in Rutherford, New Jersey, then as a draftsman for a utility company in New York. In the fall of 1920, he went to St. Louis to be an engineering advisor for a magazine called *Lumber.* In the nine months he was there, he contributed only one suggestion. Another job took him to Youngstown, Ohio, where he became an efficiency engineer for a window-sash firm; he was fired for inefficiency.

He became a "systems engineer" at a department store in Brooklyn, where he wore a bowler hat, carried a stopwatch, and made a general nuisance of himself as he attempted to develop a better system for the salespeople's process of making change for the customers. He then tried his hand at being an insurance company investigator, inspecting burnt industrial equipment for indications of arson. His most ridiculous job required that he demonstrate a motorized garden cultivator to potential clients in West Virginia. Once, when he tried to show how the machine worked in somebody's garden, he managed only

to rip up a row of cucumbers. He was dismissed.

Perhaps it was Calder's incompetence and bad luck in so many different jobs that persuaded him that art might not be such a bad occupation after all. Stirling, feeling fatherly concern for Sandy's inability to make a career for himself as an engineer, suggested that Sandy enroll in a drawing class that a friend of the family was teaching at night in a public school in midtown Manhattan. Sandy did so, and became more excited about that drawing course than about anything else he had done since graduating. He was beginning to feel uncomfortable among his fraternity brothers, who now regarded him as some sort of freak for having abandoned engineering. About this time he gave up going to parties at Stevens Institute.

Confused about what he wanted out of life, and dissatisfied with his condition, Calder suddenly felt an urge to travel. In the spring of 1922, he heard about a passenger ship, the *H. F. Alexander,* that was sailing for San Francisco and Hawaii, and needed a crew. He signed up as a fireman in the boiler room. In June, the ship—which carried more than 700 passengers and a crew of about 1,000—departed from New York.

At first, Calder found it hard to get used to his odd working schedule. He spent four hours in the boiler room, then eight hours at leisure, then another four hours in the boiler room, and so on. It was like squeezing two workdays into one twenty-four-hour period and, as a result of this around-the-clock pattern, Calder was often sleepy. He discovered that he liked sleeping on deck, on top of the great coils of hawser—the ropes used for towing or mooring the ship. It was on wakening from one of these slumbers that Calder saw the fiery red sunrise that left him with such an indelible impression of the universe.

By the time the ship arrived in San Francisco, Calder decided to cut short his adventure with the merchant marine and stay ashore. He spent a few days in San Francisco, which he enjoyed seeing again after seven years, then proceeded north, to Aberdeen, Washington. His sister Peggy and her husband met him in Aberdeen, then drove him back to their home near Tacoma, several hours away. Peggy now had two sons, and Sandy whiled away the summer with her family, making toys for his nephews.

Though Calder's family background and his natural talents pointed toward a career in art, he still felt duty-bound to prove himself as an engineer. In the fall, he looked for work in a logging camp near Independence, Washington, and accepted the only job that was offered him—that of timekeeper. It was hardly the kind of job that required a degree in mechanical engineering. The company provided him with a shack to live in, and he found himself in a logging camp that was full of tough, colorful characters.

Calder was fascinated by the loggers' "cable, pulley, donkey and log world." He was particularly impressed by the ingenious methods used to handle huge logs. The loggers frequently used a tall tree that was still standing to help them move fallen timber. A high-climber, outfitted with a belt, rope, ax and saw, first ascended a tall tree and sawed off the top. The top of the standing tree trunk was then crowned with a two-hundred-pound pulley, while the tree itself was stabilized by a half-dozen guy wires. A cable was run through the pulley; one end of the cable was attached to a fallen log some distance away, while the other end was attached to donkeys, which then dragged the log to the foot of the tree. It is easy to see how this seemingly complicated, but essentially simple, type of motion appealed to the future mobilist. The "cable, pulley, donkey and log world" set an example of ingenuity that Calder would always admire.

Calder, true to his previous work experience, had a falling-out with the camp foreman that prompted him to take another job at a nearby camp and spend the next three months there, helping to lay out a railroad line. That job was the most satisfactory he had held so far, because it required some use of his engineering knowledge.

But would Sandy be satisfied to be an engineer? It finally began to dawn on him that perhaps he did not want to be a professional engineer after all. Feeling restless and dissatisfied, Sandy increasingly longed to get back to studying art in New York. For a long time he had not drawn or painted anything. Then he was inspired to paint scenes of the logging camp and wrote home for paints and brushes. Since lumber was more available to him than canvas, he painted on wood.

By 1923, when Sandy resolved to be a painter, the reputation of his grandfather, who was then in his mid-seventies, had declined. Alexander Milne Calder's statue of William Penn was still a commanding presence of Philadelphia's skyline, but hardly anyone remembered the man who had sculpted the colossal figure. In the early twenties a Philadelphia woman thought of compiling a catalog of all the sculpture on City Hall. She wrote to Stirling in New York, because she was unaware that his father was still alive in Philadelphia, living alone in a room on South Broad Street. Grandfather Calder was gratified to learn of her interest in his City Hall sculptures, but, as much as he would have liked an illustrated cata-

log of them, he was unable to help. "I am not well and unfit for it," he wrote to the woman.

He died in June, 1923.

Sandy returned to New York and moved in again with his parents on East Tenth Street, in Manhattan. His father was dubious about Sandy abandoning the potentially lucrative career of an engineer, but Nanette was delighted that her son was going to take up painting. In the fall of 1923, Sandy entered the Art Students League of New York, where he studied with four of the outstanding painters then teaching in America. They were George Luks, John Sloan, Guy Pène du Bois and Boardman Robinson. All four had been represented in the 1913 Armory Show, and were considered artistic rebels, who introduced a more forceful, jarring type of realism.

Sandy started off by studying with Luks for two or three months. Luks painted portraits and athletic events in an exaggerated manner, making broad, slashing brushstrokes in the style of the seventeenth-century Dutch portraitists. He was known for his tall tales and boisterous behavior, and he relished this reputation, calling himself "the best barroom fighter in America." Luks occasionally came to school in a tipsy condition and, as Calder recalled, "we used to have a rather good time in his class."

Sandy went to John Sloan's class every evening. Sloan was a gruff, outspoken man, who specialized in painting scenes of city life—evening strollers out for a good time; young women drying their hair on a rooftop; older women on tenement fire escapes, hanging their laundry out to dry. Although Sloan himself was an often clumsy draftsman, he impressed Sandy as a good instructor—mainly because he urged students to develop their own talents rather than do things his way.

Unlike Luks and Sloan, Guy Pène du Bois painted well-to-do people, sometimes in aristocratic settings, and frequently conveyed a sense of satire. His mannequin-like women wore stylish clothing and makeup, and they appealed to Sandy because the "girls looked like wood carvings, even somewhat like toys."

Calder's fourth teacher at the League, Boardman Robinson, was a big, likable man with red hair and beard who had been a newspaper illustrator. Calder considered him an "excellent teacher." It was Robinson who taught Sandy to draw with "a pen and a single line," capturing the essence of subjects by concentrating on their most expressive outlines. Often, while riding the subway to and from school, Sandy carried a sheet of paper, folded into eight rectangles to fit into his pocket, and whiled away the time sketching other riders. "I seemed to have a knack for doing it with a single line," he said later.

In his drawings, Calder economized on lines, and in his daily life, he economized on everything involving money. He was frugal by nature and kept a watchful eye over every penny that came his way. He made a practice of buying used canvases at the League because it was cheaper to paint over someone else's work than to start out with a brand-new canvas.

Sandy frequently accompanied a fellow student on field trips to paint the city. He didn't carry an easel because he liked to attach his canvas, with nails and string, to any available fence or post that provided support. Eventually, the two students started going out in the evening to paint, and Sandy believed he was acquiring some skill in rendering artificial lights. It was about this time that he painted an evening view of the old Madison Square Garden building, garishly illuminated and decked out with patriotic bunting for the 1924 Democratic National Convention.

Calder also managed to get occasional freelance work as a cartoonist for *The National Police Gazette,* an illustrated weekly magazine devoted to sports and entertainment news. The editor was enthusiastic about Sandy's single-line drawings, and commissioned him to do a half-page of sketches. Sandy received twenty dollars for each half page, a good deal of money at that time for a beginning artist.

Sandy's *Police Gazette* assignments led him all over the city. Among the subjects he sketched were Coney Island, the annual horse show and a track-and-field star—Paavo Nurmi, the Finnish "wonder runner," who won several events in both the 1920 and 1924 Olympics. The half-page layouts usually consisted of nine or so "action sketches" in pen-and-ink, showing various aspects of an event, and were usually accompanied by sassy captions. Sandy's sketches for the *Police Gazette* indicate that he was a brilliant illustrator and caricaturist. He had a sharp eye and a quick hand, which enabled him to jot down the essential forms and movements of his wide range of animated subjects.

When the Ringling Brothers and Barnum & Bailey Circus came to Madison Square Garden, Sandy spent two exhilarating weeks sketching the various acts and animals. He was fascinated by the vast space of the circus, and impressed by the way a single spotlight could focus attention on a small area. There was a famous aerial gymnast, Lillian Leitzel, who did one hundred "twists," somersaulting her body while hanging by one wrist from a rope at a dizzying height.

"What I loved," Sandy said, "was the spotlight on her and the rest in obscurity!" He attended so many performances that he could tell from the music what act was coming on. The music sometimes set him scampering from one level to another to get the best possible view of each act.

Although he spent two weeks at the circus, Sandy published only the usual half-page of sketches in the *Police Gazette*. But the experience continued to inspire him for a great many years,

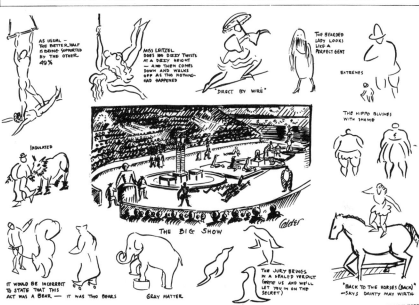

ALL THE WONDERS OF THE WORLD IN THREE RINGS—SOME IMPRESSIONISTIC SKETCHES OF THE BARNUM-RINGLING CIRCUS WHILE IT WAS SHOWING IN NEW YORK, Recently, in Madison Square Garden, Just Prior to the Demolition of that Historic Amphitheatre. The "Big Show" Is the Best Sort of Spring Tonic for the Grown-ups As Well As the Youngsters. It Preserves Some of the Romance of Youth that the Rush and Bustle of City Life So Soon Impair or Destroy. Calder Shows Us Not Only the Main Show, but the Freaks of the Side-show.

and resulted in numerous drawings and sculptures of acrobats, clowns, trained animals and other circus themes. His zest for the circus was so great that, in time, he would be ringmaster of his own miniature circus, "just for the fun of it."

Sandy made several efforts to make a living as an artist in New York, but without much luck. In the spring of 1926, he decided to go to Paris. From all he had heard, it was the ideal city if one wanted to be an artist. In June, he managed to work his way to Europe by getting a job as an ordinary sailor on a British freighter, sailing from Hoboken. At age twenty-seven, he was embarking on a voyage that would change his life.

OPPOSITE: Drawing from *The National Police Gazette*, February 21, 1925.
LEFT: *Circus*, 1926. Oil painting, 69" x 83". Collection Margaret Calder Hayes, Berkeley, California.
ABOVE: Drawing from *The National Police Gazette*, May 23, 1925.

25

4 SANDY KNEW NO ONE WHEN HE ARRIVED IN PARIS. Though the city bubbled with artistic activity, he was not especially receptive to any new ideas in the air. Still, he could not help but be stimulated by the sights and the people of the city.

There are some periods in history when one city predominates as a center of artistic activity. In the 1920s that city was Paris. The "city of light" had no peer as a cultural capital. Paris, having recovered from World War I, still retained a great deal of its old charm—in large part because of its eighteenth- and nineteenth-century buildings. But the spirit of the city was optimistic, even exuberant, and inspired a receptive attitude to anything that was lively and experimental. Like a magnet, Paris attracted outstanding artists from all over the world.

No people flocked to Paris in greater numbers than the Americans. During the 1920s, nearly 35,000 Americans lived there. They went for any number of reasons—adventure, culture, work, a good time. The city offered countless diversions and the cost of living was relatively low. Wine flowed freely in France, while the United States had gone dry because of Prohibition. Many Americans felt freer and more liberated in Paris than in puritanical America. In short, Americans were enchanted by Paris and the infatuation was mutual. The French adored the Americans for their simplicity, liveliness and, perhaps most of

all, their jazz. The entire decade became known as the "jazz age."

Some of the most sensational entertainers in Paris were Americans. The biggest American star in the French music halls was unquestionably Josephine Baker—a tall, slim and extraordi-

The Hostess, 1928. Wire sculpture, 11½" h. The Museum of Modern Art, New York; gift of Edward M. M. Warburg.

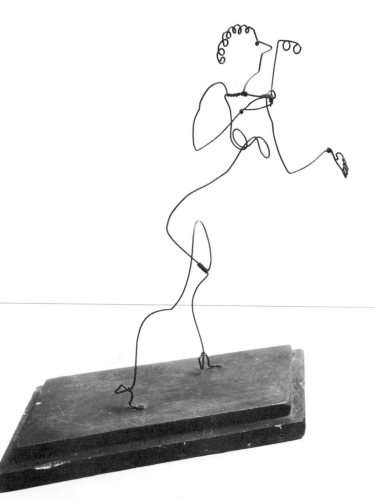

narily beautiful black woman from St. Louis, who created a sensation in 1925 when she made her debut at the Théâtre des Champs-Elysées. Singing and dancing almost entirely in the nude, she was carried onto the stage—upside down and doing the splits—or lowered from the ceiling on a mirrored platform, wearing nothing but a few flamingo feathers or a bunch of bananas around her hips. Paris went crazy over this "black Venus" and "most beautiful panther."

During the twenties, Americans made a sig-

Soda Fountain, 1928. Wire sculpture, 10³/₄" h. The Museum of Modern Art, New York; gift of the artist.

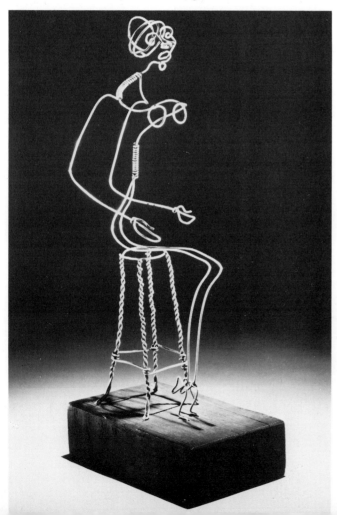

Josephine Baker, 1927–29. Wire sculpture, 22³/₈" x 9³/₄". The Museum of Modern Art, New York; gift of the artist.

The black American singer and dancer was the sensation of Parisian music halls.

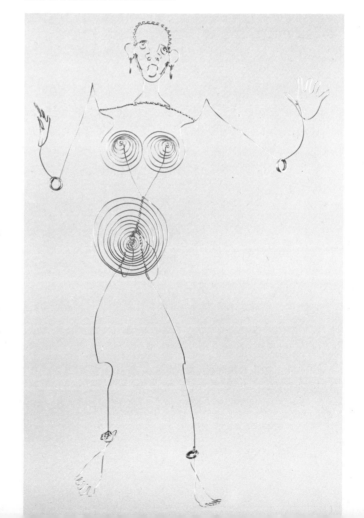

nificant contribution to the cultural life of Paris. If one takes into account all the exciting things that were being done in Paris by people from Spain, Russia, the Netherlands, Japan, and, of course, France itself, it is easy to understand why young artists like Calder felt the necessity to be in the French capital.

In the beginning, Sandy stayed at the Hôtel de Versailles in Montparnasse, an inexpensive section of Paris that was popular with visiting Americans. His hotel room was small, but on a high floor with a pleasant view overlooking the rooftops of Paris. Sandy did not know what to do with himself during his first days in the city. He attended some drawing classes at the Académie de la Grande Chaumière, but much of the time he wandered the streets aimlessly. Often he just sat on a sidewalk bench and watched the people walking past him. One day he was seated on a bench outside the Dôme, a Montparnasse café popular with artists, when he recognized an American painter he had known in New York. Together they made the rounds of a few cafés. Eventually Sandy acquired the habit of going to a café whenever he wanted a bit of social activity. In time, he met many people and made a few friends.

Before long, Sandy rented a room in a building on Rue Daguerre, also in the Montparnasse section. The room, which was located in the rear of the building, one flight up, was just barely adequate for living and working. But Calder was thrilled to have his own studio in Paris. Best of all, for the first time in his life, he had his own skylight. The only drawback to the place was the poor heating system. The radiator, he complained, was "barely warm enough to dry a handkerchief."

One could live in Paris with little money in those days. Sandy's mother sent him seventy-five dollars a month, almost enough to make ends meet. For additional income, he found occasional odd jobs. He worked as a free-lance illustrator, sketching portraits of visiting Americans for the Paris *Herald Tribune,* and he made stylish cartoons for a weekly periodical called *Le Boulevardier.* He also did a series of drawings promoting the transatlantic sailings of the Holland-America Line.

While he still wanted to be a painter, Sandy spent an increasing amount of time fashioning small animals out of wood and wire. He was partly inspired by a ready-made set of circus toys that he had worked with some time before. That set contained some clowns with slotted feet and clawlike hands that enabled them to dangle from a miniature ladder by a hand or foot. Sandy rigged up some strings so that one of the clowns could be made to jump onto the back of a toy elephant. The new animals that he now made had movable parts, and were articulated in such a way that they could perform a variety of actions. He enjoyed making these whimsical creatures for his own pleasure, and did not look upon them as serious works of art.

One day a friend stopped by the studio, examined the animals, and asked Sandy why he did not eliminate the wood and make them entirely out of wire. Grateful for this idea, Sandy proceeded to make his first all-wire figure, a forty-inch-high representation of Josephine Baker (page 27). Although he had never seen her perform, he portrayed her in a way that caricatured her public image. What is most remarkable is that he was able to give her a convincing three-dimensionality by using a single piece of wire; the sculpture suggests that he was deliberately translating one of his single-line drawings into three dimensions. He bent the wire this way and that so that it became fingers, toes, curled hair, eyes (with a little loop to indicate the irises) and nose (with a pair of little loops to indicate nostrils). He coiled the wire into spiraling beehive-like forms to represent her breasts and belly. As originally conceived, "Josephine Baker" was to dangle from the ceiling by a thread which would let the sculpture vibrate ever so slightly, creating the illusion of a springy, buoyant figure.

Sandy kept himself so busy working on his sculpture and toys, and palling around with his circle of friends, that he remained indifferent to the rest of the world. One evening in May 1927, Sandy was sitting with friends at the Dôme when someone called out: "Lindbergh is due at Le Bourget." Sandy and his friends scrambled into taxis to get to the airport in time to witness this historic event. Captain Charles A. Lindbergh, a young American airmail pilot, was making the first solo, nonstop transatlantic flight from New York to Paris, and the entire world held its breath while waiting to see whether his single-propeller airplane, only twenty-seven feet long, would reach its destination. Thousands of people flocked to Le Bourget Airport and, when Lindbergh finally touched down after his thirty-three-and-one-half-hour flight, he received a hero's welcome. Inexplicably, Sandy failed to witness the actual landing. "I guess he came down behind us," he explained many years later.

Sandy continued to construct his articulated figures and, in the spring of 1927, he struck up a friendship with a French artist, associated with *Le Boulevardier,* who became enthusiastic about the miniature circus. The Frenchman brought his friends, including circus critics, to Calder's studio. What Sandy had begun as a hobby to entertain himself gradually developed into full-fledged performances, and the word-of-mouth news about Calder's little circus spread quickly throughout Montparnasse.

29

Sandy conducted the performances on his studio floor. The audience crowded onto a low studio bed. Sandy then unrolled a bit of green carpet, laid out a ring, and erected some poles to support the trapezes for the aerial acts. A record—usually the popular song "Ramona"—was placed on the phonograph. Sandy, speaking as the ringmaster, announced: "Mesdames et Messieurs, je vous présente. . . ." and the performance began.

Rag Animal Toys, undated. Cloth, wire and string, approx. 6" h.

To keep his circus lively, Sandy frequently added new performers and acts. When one of his early visitors, a circus critic, demanded that Sandy place a net under his trapeze act for greater authenticity, he immediately did so. As the circus became increasingly popular, it attracted distinguished visitors—including Paul Fratellini, one of three brothers of a famous family of Italian circus clowns. Fratellini was very taken with the dog in the circus, so Sandy devised a larger version—a dachshund made out of rubber tubing and christened Miss Tamara—and presented it to Fratellini. Miss Tamara, who

wagged her tail as she wobbled about on spoke-like legs, remained part of the Fratellini circus act for many years.

Meanwhile, some people encouraged Calder to design articulated toys that could be mass-produced, assuring him that he could make a fortune in the toy industry. So in addition to producing circus figures in wire, wood, tin and leather, Calder thought about devising commercial toys.

By the time Sandy returned to the United States in the fall of 1927, his circus gear filled two suitcases. Once he had resettled in New York, he made a brief trip out to Oshkosh, Wisconsin, where he visited a toy company and worked out an agreement to design some "action toys." The company eventually manufactured about a dozen toys based on Sandy's models. Most of them were "pull" toys on wheels, and all were made of painted wood with movable parts. According to the manufacturer's advertisement, "Both grownups and youngsters are fascinated by their lifelike action." There was a Duckie Toddler that had "the action of a scared duck-

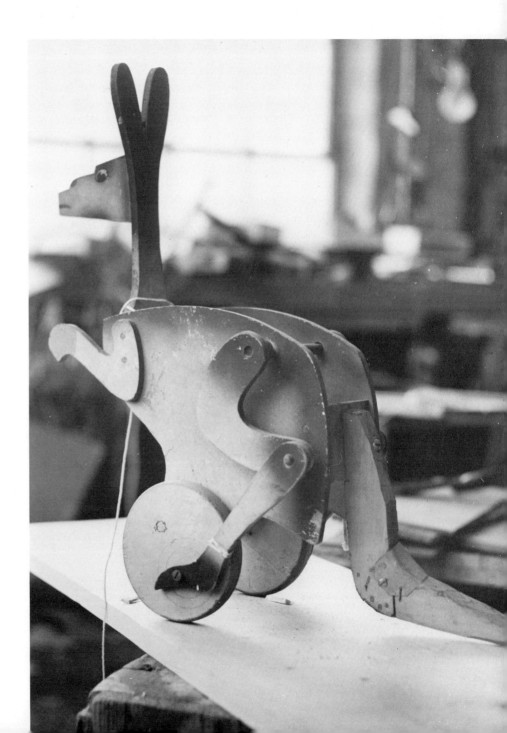

Kangaroo, 1927. Wooden toy, 20" h.
This jaunty marsupial, which goes through hopping motions when the wheels revolve, is one of several Calder-designed "action toys" produced by the Gould Manufacturing Company in Oshkosh, Wisconsin.

ling," a Quackie Toddler that "claps its bill with a loud quack," and a sixteen-and-one-half-inch-long goldfish that "wiggles like a swimming fish." There were also a hopping kangaroo and a skating bear. "All are substantially constructed, attractively colored and will stand plenty of 'knocking' around," the advertisement claimed. The company credited the design to: "Alexander Calder of New York and Paris." For the next few years, Calder's "action toys" brought him a royalty of about fifty dollars a month.

Calder had his first one-man show of sculpture in February 1928, at the Weyhe Gallery in New York. He exhibited about fifteen objects, mostly wire animals and people. And he constructed a special sign to hang in the window—a wire figure of an acrobat, hanging by the knees and holding a sign that spelled out in wire letters: "Wire sculpture by Calder." The wire objects were tagged at ten to twenty dollars but, even at those low prices, he was able to sell only two or three things.

Stirling Calder visited the show and was amused by the wire objects. But, Sandy reported, his father thought "they were too sharp to be caressed and fondled as one could do with small bronzes." Stirling, at that time, was engaged in producing four statues to adorn the building of the I. Miller shoe company in New York. The statues represented famous perform-ers in their most celebrated roles: Film star Mary Pickford as Little Lord Fauntleroy, actress Ethel Barrymore as Ophelia, Broadway musical-comedy star Marilyn Miller as Sunny, and opera singer Rosa Ponselle as Norma. The four women had been the winners in a popularity contest conducted among theatregoers. During the month of February, Stirling received considerable attention for his study of Ethel Barrymore, while hardly anyone took notice of Sandy's portrait in wire of Josephine Baker.

Sandy spent the winter in a cozy apartment overlooking Charles Street and Seventh Avenue in Greenwich Village. He devoted most of his time to carving wood sculpture; but while he made some satisfactory works in this medium, few of his carved wood pieces match the brilliance and ingenuity of his wire constructions. Luckily, he did find time to make two wire constructions that turned out to be among his most delightful works.

These were "Spring" (page 112) and "Romulus and Remus" (page 113). Both are larger-than-life-size works, suggesting three-dimensional line drawings, and the wire is bent with a marvelous fluidity and spontaneity. More than most of his wire pieces, they demonstrate his masterful economy of line and his sly wit. "Spring" is a ninety-four-and-one-half-inch-high young woman, outlined in wire, with a pointy nose and chin, and a squiggly lock of hair. Most artists conventionally symbolize spring as a shapely creature just entering the full bloom of womanhood. Calder's "Spring" is more like an anemic adolescent. Her ungainliness makes her amusing—and also touching.

"Romulus and Remus" is Calder's droll interpretation of the legendary twins who were said to have founded Rome after being adopted and suckled by a she-wolf. The she-wolf, in Sandy's hands, became eleven feet long. Far from looking fierce, she has the most benign expression possible. The infant boys, with their wide-open mouths, obviously have only one thing on their minds—nourishing wolf milk. Calder used wooden and rubber doorstops, purchased at the five-and-ten, to serve as the nipples of the she-wolf and the penises of the boys. Both "Spring" and "Romulus and Remus" demonstrate Calder's humorous treatment of classical subjects.

In the spring of 1928, Calder exhibited the two constructions in a show organized by the Society of Independent Artists at the old Waldorf Hotel, then located on Thirty-fourth Street. The following year he showed them again at the Salon des Indépendants in Paris, where they were well received, if not taken very seriously as art. After that, they were crushed flat and stored in a warehouse where they remained, all but completely forgotten, for thirty-five years.

Calder returned to Paris in November 1928, and took a new ground-floor studio on Rue Cels, a few blocks away from his old place on Rue Daguerre. By now he was a pretty familiar figure on the Left Bank. Because of his unconventional dressing habits, he was not an easy figure to miss or forget. He sometimes wore a bright-orange tweed suit and a ribboned straw hat, an outfit that inspired some people to call him "the cantaloupe with the straw hat." He had acquired an orange bicycle and took to pedaling around Paris in gray knickers and bright red socks. Once, when he had a cold, he startled Parisians by suspending a piece of camphor under his nose by a wire that looped around his ears.

Sandy hurried off to the Dome, where he hoped to encounter some old chums. He not only saw people he knew, but was also introduced to one of the celebrities of Paris—Jules Pascin, the Bulgarian-born painter who personified the bohemian artist. Pascin, then in his early forties, led a vigorously dissolute life, and was known for wild parties, excessive drinking and battles with women friends. He was a homely man, but thoroughly entertaining. Although he described himself as "the unhappiest man in the world," his stories of the miserable abuses he had suffered at the hands of dealers and mistresses were so funny that they only increased his popularity. He drew superbly and was considered a daring

33

artist at the time for his erotic pictures of women sprawled on beds and chairs. He and Sandy took a liking to each other and, the following week, Sandy invited Pascin to a party at his studio. Pascin accepted the invitation, adding that he would be bringing about forty people.

Sandy later attended many of Pascin's parties,

frantic affairs during which nearly everyone drank too much. In time, Sandy and Pascin exchanged artworks. Pascin offered a caricature, showing Sandy on horseback and drawn in a manner that mimics Calder's own style of single-line drawing. In return, Sandy gave Pascin one of his wire figures of Josephine Baker.

Pascin, being widely known in the Paris art world, was a powerful ally and played an instrumental part in getting Calder his first one-man show in Paris at the Galerie Billiet in January 1929. He also agreed to write a preface for the gallery brochure. While drinking at a café table

The Horse, 1928. Wood sculpture, walnut, 15½" x 34¾". The Museum of Modern Art, New York; acquired through the Lillie P. Bliss Bequest.

This work is both carved and constructed, the animal's trunk wedged into separately cut pairs of legs. Calder employed similar joinings in his later metal stabiles.

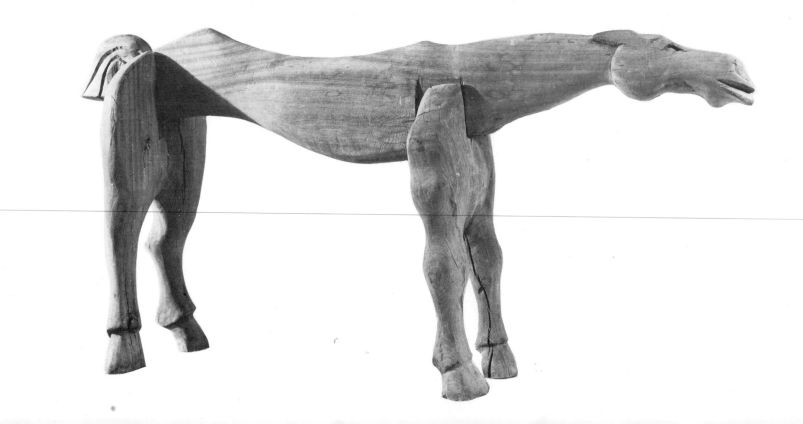

at La Coupole, Pascin scrawled in nearly illegible French the following statement:

By I don't know what miracle I became a member of a leading American art group. A society of very successful painters and sculptors, Hoho! Hoho! the luck of a wandering painter. The same luck brought me a meeting with the father, Stirling Calder. Away from New York where our last exhibition took place, I cannot judge our effort, but in any case, I swear to you that Mr. Stirling Calder, who is one of our best American sculptors, is also the handsomest man of our society. Back in Paris, I met his son Sandy Calder, who disappointed me deeply at first sight. He is less handsome than his Papa! Really. But, faced with his works, I know that he will very soon be accepted, in spite of his ugly mug, and he will exhibit with shattering success beside his papa and other great artists like me, Pascin, who tells you this . . . !

Calder's show contained several pieces of carved wood sculpture and a number of wire con-

Cow, 1929. Wire sculpture, 6½″ x 16″. The Museum of Modern Art, New York; gift of Edward M. M. Warburg.

As the tail is lifted, a small hook releases the coiled mound of dung.

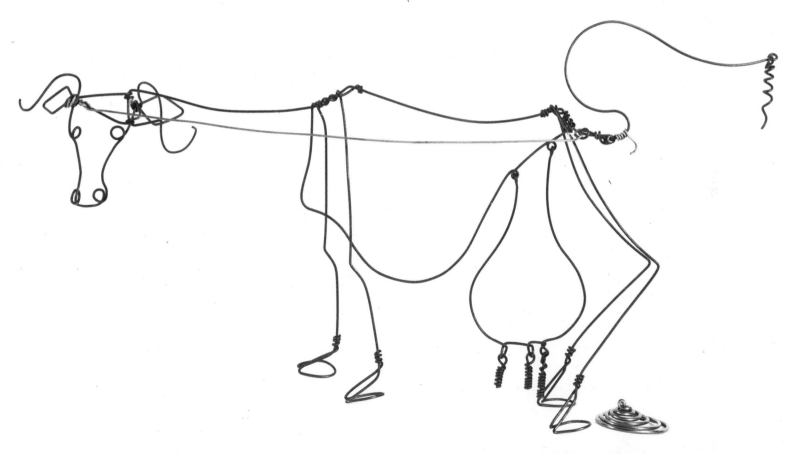

structions. Probably the most comic piece of this period was the wire "Acrobats" (page 37), showing an accident-prone pair of tumblers. As the topmost man performs a handstand on the head of his partner, he loses his balance and his hand slips down over the eyes of his partner, who stoically bends at the knees to keep from tottering.

The show received a favorable review in the Paris *Herald Tribune*. The art critic saw little originality in the wood sculpture, but he raved over the wire pieces, calling them "a new and decidedly interesting means of expressing appreciable serio-comic ideas." Calder's method of modeling wire, the critic explained, was to determine the most significant lines, as if he were drawing with a pen. "The longer one observes it," the critic concluded, "the more one is convinced of the fact that here is a new language."

In April 1929, Sandy was in Berlin, where he had been invited to have another one-man gallery show. He brought with him a bundle of fifteen to twenty wire sculptures, but he managed to sell only one piece, a wire dachshund. Nevertheless, the show was reviewed with enthusiasm by a German art critic who wrote:

One experiences a rare pleasure in viewing the work of an American, Alexander Calder, sculptor . . . an extraordinary man. . . . Calder has studied his creatures so carefully: a mule stretching his head forward, a bellowing dog with stiffened knees, a singer with an inflated diaphragm reading from a sheet of music, a small man and a large woman bent over as they run home through the rain. . . .

One can regard these wire creatures as one wishes—as toys or as works of art. More than anything else, one would like to take them home to hang on the wall.

Having received a good deal of coverage in the German press, Sandy returned to Paris, where his arrival was noted by the Paris *Herald Tribune*: "Alexander (Sandy) Calder, one of the best-known and most frequent American visitors to Montparnasse, just drove in from Berlin on his pet bicycle, adorned in the habitual sailor trousers and orange socks, loaded down with his wire horses and wooden cows." He seemed—to the *Herald Tribune* reporter—to be "in rollicking good spirits," as if his Berlin show had been a great success.

Late in April, Gustave Fréjaville, a critic of Paris music halls and circuses, wrote a glowing appraisal of Sandy's live circus performances for the newspaper *Comoedia*. That article apparently helped inspire the Pathé newsreel company to visit Calder's studio for a documentary film called *Artist*.

In spite of the critical acclaim, Sandy was running out of money. In June, he decided to book passage to New York on the *De Grasse*. And this

turned out to be his most momentous boat ride since he saw the fiery red sun bob out of the Guatemalan waters seven years earlier.

What caught Sandy's eye on this voyage was the windblown hair of a young woman, as she promenaded with an elderly man on the deck. Sandy, who was walking behind, overtook them but was unable to get a good look at the woman's face. On his next turn around the deck, he reversed his direction in order to confront the couple face-to-face. As he drew near, he noticed that the woman had plump cheeks and blue eyes. Sandy greeted them with a hearty "Good evening!" The woman ignored him, and her companion snorted contemptuously.

That evening, after dinner, there was a formal dance on the ship. Sandy, feeling uncomfortable in his tuxedo, recognized the young woman who had so pointedly ignored him that afternoon. He asked her for a dance and, to his surprise, she accepted. As he led her around the dance floor, he tried not to bruise her feet while amusing her with chitchat. She asked what he did for a living and he replied, "I'm a wire sculptor."

She did not have the faintest idea what he meant but, not wanting to appear stupid, she

Acrobats, 1929. Wire sculpture, 35" x 22". Menil Foundation Collection, Houston, Texas.

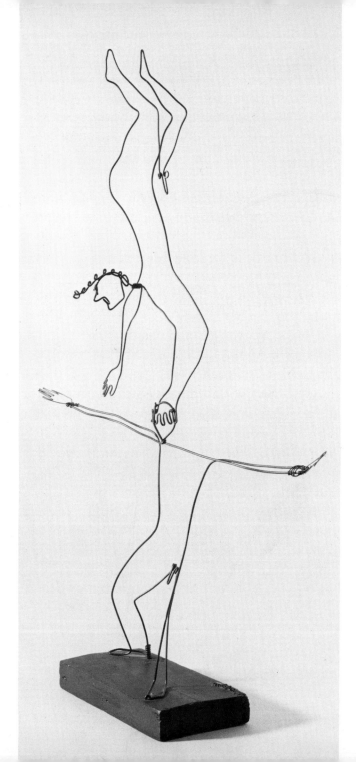

managed to keep quiet and look nonchalant. She introduced herself as Louisa James, from Concord, Massachusetts. She was traveling with her father, Edward Holton James, who had taken her to Europe to see the sights and to acquire a smattering of culture. She also had hoped to meet some young men of good breeding, but the only Europeans she encountered were cabdrivers, doormen and waiters. She was distantly related to the eminent novelist, Henry James, and his brother William, the equally famous psychologist and philosopher. But both of her illustrious granduncles were long dead, and of no use in advancing her social career.

When Louisa reported Sandy's occupation to her father, Mr. James was puzzled and disapproving. But he was afflicted with a severe case of asthma during the voyage and kept to his cabin. Consequently, Louisa spent a lot of time with Sandy, playing deck tennis or watching flying fish.

A week or so after the boat docked in New York, Louisa invited Sandy to visit her and her sister Mary, at their summer cottage on Cape Cod. Sandy enjoyed staying so close to the ocean. He liked swimming and, of course, ate heartily throughout his visit. Later, when he had installed himself in his father's studio on East Fourteenth Street in Manhattan, Louisa paid him

a visit. He had just constructed one of his wire animals and was delighted when Louisa was able to recognize it as a horse. Sandy realized she had an eye for art!

That fall, Sandy shared an apartment in a fashionable section of Manhattan. His roommate, a man in the book-publishing business, took a keen interest in Sandy's circus and helped make additional performers and acts. They created a mustachioed, stern-looking lion tamer, who brandished a whip and gun and had long wire arms that could be manipulated at a distance by strings. They also constructed a rousing chariot-race act, inspired by the races Sandy had witnessed as a child in Pasadena. The chariots were made of metal and moved on wooden wheels. Each chariot was drawn by a pair of horses, made of spindly wire legs, round wooden trunks, arched metal necks and leather or twine tails. The charioteers were garbed in colorful cloth togas and headbands.

The stock market crashed during the last week of October 1929, signaling the end of prosperous times and the beginning of what became known as the Great Depression. Billions of dollars virtually vanished in the biggest economic collapse of

The Circus, c. 1932. Ink drawing, 20¼" x 29¼". Collection Mr. and Mrs. Klaus G. Perls, New York.

the century. Many people lost their jobs and almost starved for lack of money. But Sandy, who tinkered away at his miniature circus, scarcely noticed the catastrophe all around him.

In December, he exhibited his work at the Fifty-sixth Street Galleries. There were about an equal number of wood and wire sculptures in the show. Although Sandy placed higher value on the wood pieces, it is the wire works that are more original and more prized today. Among these were "The Brass Family" (*left*), featuring a giant strong man who supports a human pyramid of six acrobats, and "Soda Fountain" (page 27), representing a stylish young woman perched on an ice-cream parlor stool. The prices, by today's standards, were modest: "The Brass Family" was tagged at five hundred dollars and "Soda Fountain" went unsold at fifty dollars.

The exhibition brochure contained an excerpt from a review of Calder's previous New York show, written by Murdock Pemberton, art critic of *The New Yorker* magazine. Pemberton predicted:

Calder is nothing for your grandmother but we imagine he will be the choice of your sons. He makes a mockery of the

The Brass Family, 1929. Wire sculpture, brass, 64" x 41" x 8 1/2". Whitney Museum of American Art, New York; gift of the artist.

old-fashioned frozen-stone school of sculpture and comes nearer to life in his creations than do nine-tenths of the serious stone-cutters. Some of his wood elephants and tin animals are masterpieces of motion and balance, and his cow is a cow with all of her pathos left in.

In reviewing Calder's current show, Pemberton exclaimed:

We have raved about Calder every time he has appeared on the horizon . . . . . With an unbroken wire for his stock in trade, he is held to the essentials. His line must be perfect, his economy rigid, and his composition and balance all that the laws of gravity demand. Calder gets more grace and beauty into the left hind leg of his lion than many old-timers do with a square yard of canvas and a pail of paint.

Pemberton was less responsive to Sandy's toys and paintings.

Pell-mell he throws out his sparks; some of them take fire and others do not. We are not sure, though, that any other method would work for Mr. Calder. Deliberation and studiousness would not enrich his output, we feel certain.

In its "The Talk of the Town" section, *The New Yorker* also took note of Calder's circus:

You can't buy tickets to it, but people who have seen it say it is worth getting a bid to a private showing. . . . Mr. Calder sits on the floor, beside a miniature tanbark ring, and is very busy. He keeps seventy performers doing incredible things with their wire joints and felt bodies—trapeze artists, high-divers, bareback riders, clowns, lions, horses and dogs. The tricks are often ingeniously contrived. For example, the horses are mounted on a disc which Mr. Calder can whirl madly, by turning the handle of an old eggbeater. At the proper moment, a spring or something is released, a bareback rider in ballet skirts flies through the air, bursts through a hoop, and lands astride a horse. People scream. Calder seldom misses. For faint hearts, a net is spread beneath the trapeze performers. Clowns tumble about the ring, poodles sit up, a hoochie-coochie dancer brings down the house. It all lasts about two hours, and nobody ever walks out or even gets restive.

Sandy managed to sell enough work to enable him to return to Paris the following March. This time, he and his circus—which now filled five trunks—crossed the ocean on a Spanish freighter that departed from Brooklyn. Louisa was unable to see him off, but her sister Mary accompanied Sandy's mother to Brooklyn to wish him "bon voyage."

Back in Paris, Sandy rented a new studio at 7 Villa Brune, in the same section of the city as before. He hastened to La Coupole, only to discover that the old gang that used to hang out there had broken up. Some of his friends now patronized another café, La Rotonde, across the street.

One of the few faces Sandy recognized at La Coupole belonged to Jules Pascin. But Pascin was gloomier than ever and Sandy preferred to avoid him. During the first week of June, Pascin secluded himself in his studio and slashed his wrists. As death proved too slow in coming, he hanged himself. When Sandy heard the news, he was shocked.

Meanwhile, Louisa spent most of the summer in Europe, first touring Ireland on a bicycle, then finally spending a few weeks in Paris. One of the first things she did was contact Sandy. He was delighted to see her again and flattered by her attention. It was obvious they had become extremely fond of one another, but for the moment at least, Sandy was unwilling to assume the responsibilities of marriage.

Sandy was running low on money again. To pay his rent, he staged a series of circus performances in his studio. He collected planks and boxes in order to construct bleachers, and he charged admission. As many as thirty people an evening paid to see the circus.

BELOW: At this 1943 circus performance in New York, Sandy presented his ever-suspenseful chariot race, pulling the tin chariots around the arena by strings. The caged lion has a stuffed cloth head, a wire body and a mane of gold yarn.

OPPOSITE: A large, talented cast of aerialists, clowns and trained animals constituted Sandy's miniature circus. With only a few pieces of cloth, a couple of poles and guy wires, he evoked the vast space inside a circus tent.

The miniature circus contained almost all of the customary attractions. There was a sword-swallower, a pair of Japanese wrestlers, a bearded lady, a parachuting clown, a cowboy, a man on stilts and Rigoulot, the strong man, who was made of wire and articulated in such a way that he could bend over, pick up a barbell and lift it high above his head. A formidable-looking prima donna in a long, peach-colored gown sang an operatic aria; as she sang, "doves" fluttered downward and settled upon her shoulders. The doves were actually little bits of white paper with tiny weights attached; the bits of paper were strung on thin, slightly coiled wires which Sandy jiggled until the doves reached the shoulders of the bejeweled soprano.

To complement the human performers, there were numerous talented animals—many horses, a camel, a kangaroo, a blue elephant with white pipe-cleaners for tusks, and even a pair of seals that tossed a ball back and forth between their cork noses.

As in a real circus, there was always the element of risk. A bareback rider might fall off the horse, and a jumping dog might not make it through the paper hoop. Calder deliberately included a few acts that repeatedly "failed." The most thrilling, perhaps, was the trapeze act in which the female aerialist swung from one tra-peze, connected her wire feet with a second trapeze, then leaped to a third. She usually fell, but luckily landed in the safety net. Sometimes Sandy picked her up and moved her to a spot where she could dangle more perilously from a torn part of the net.

The wit and ingenuity of Sandy's circus enchanted audiences wherever it was presented. The circus brought Sandy his first fame. By the end of 1930, he was thirty-two years old and widely known in Paris as an offbeat sort of entertainer. But he had yet to make his mark as a "serious" artist.

Sandy couldn't have cared less about being a "serious" artist. He was a boisterous clown at heart, and totally absorbed in the circus world he had created for himself. So he continued to blow his whistle, signaling the start of another performance. Monsieur Loyal, the ringmaster, entered the ring, turned around and greeted the audience. His head consisted of a cork, painted with facial features. He wore a top hat and tuxedo, and he held a bullhorn in one hand. Sandy could make the ringmaster's arms move by manipulating a couple of strings that ran through a wire loop in front of Monsieur Loyal's mouth. Sandy pulled the bullhorn to Monsieur Loyal's lips and, in a theatrical voice, announced: "Mesdames et messieurs, je vous présente. . . ."

ONE EVENING IN THE FALL OF 1930, a tall, stony-faced stranger showed up at Calder's studio to attend a performance of the circus. His manner was aloof and almost forbidding as he observed the proceedings with intense interest. Sandy was so preoccupied with getting his contraptions together that he didn't even notice the man. But William Einstein, Sandy's American friend who was operating the phonograph for him, instantly realized that the spectacled stranger was none other than the Dutch painter Piet Mondrian.

Mondrian, then fifty-eight years old, was a crotchety, dandyish bachelor. He had the reputation of an eccentric intellectual, who whiled away his time painting nothing but straight black lines and colored rectangles on white canvas. Most people did not understand his work; and some who did found it cold and cerebral. Many years afterward Mondrian would be acclaimed internationally as one of the most important artists of the twentieth century.

After the circus performance Einstein, who was also a painter, rushed across the room to introduce himself to Mondrian. A few days later, Einstein reported that he had visited the Dutchman's studio. He gave a glowing account of the visit and insisted that Sandy, too, should meet Mondrian. Sandy became curious. What was so special about this artist, he wondered?

No one dropped in on Mondrian uninvited, so Einstein applied for another invitation and, after it was received, the two Americans set out for the nearby Rue de Départ, where Mondrian occupied a third-floor studio overlooking the railroad tracks of the Montparnasse train station. Mondrian, despite his stern-looking appearance and old-fashioned formality, greeted them cordially and led them into his quarters. His studio was so orderly that it could have been a three-dimensional version of one of his paintings. Mondrian applied the same principles of design and rationality to his daily life as to his art. On the walls, he had tacked up large rectangles of cardboard, painted in the primary colors—red, yellow and blue—that he used on his canvases. The wicker armchairs were painted white and the phonograph was painted bright red. On a table near the door, Mondrian kept a vase containing a single tulip, a flower that virtually symbolized his native Holland. However, the flower was artificial and, since Mondrian could not abide the color green, he had painted the leaves white.

Mondrian's friends and admirers tolerated his many idiosyncrasies because they believed him to be a genius. His paintings expressed a new vision, one that pushed art beyond the literal representation of everyday reality. When he chose to, Mondrian could draw flowers, trees and

5

buildings as elegantly as any other outstanding draftsman. But he preferred to assemble abstract shapes and colors in such a way that they became visually and emotionally satisfying, while, at the same time, expressing an idealized sense of order.

Sandy was greatly impressed—both by the man and his art. He had no difficulty responding to the rhythmic, harmonious qualities of Mondrian's art. He even had the audacity to suggest to Mondrian, "Your rectangles should vibrate and oscillate."

Mondrian shook his head and said coldly, "No, it is not necessary, my painting is already very fast." To his way of thinking, no actual movement was needed since he had scrupulously balanced his lines, rectangles and colors in such a way that there was virtually nothing static about the compositions.

This meeting with Mondrian was one of the most crucial events in Calder's artistic development. Mondrian was the first artist, at least in Sandy's eyes, who deliberately sought to rede-

Piet Mondrian, *Lozenge in Red, Yellow and Blue*, c. 1925. Oil painting, 40" x 40". National Gallery of Art, Washington, D.C.; gift of Herbert and Nannette Rothschild.

Because Mondrian valued pure forms and colors, he generally restricted himself to straight lines and the primary colors—red, yellow, blue along with black, white and gray. While this painting appears to include ten rectangles, only one of them is complete.

fine art, casting off the traditions of the past to invent something genuinely new. Sandy recognized that Mondrian's work was helping to establish new ways of seeing, thinking and feeling about art.

"This one visit," Calder said many years later, "gave me a shock that started things." Though he often heard the word "modern," he had seldom taken it to mean "abstract." It now dawned on him that abstraction was the most modern kind of art that one could make. So Calder determined that he, too, would be an abstract artist.

He returned to his studio and began to experiment. His first attempts at abstract painting were far from successful, but he did succeed in turning out several outstanding line drawings. Some of the black-and-white, pen-and-ink drawings clearly refer to the universe, resembling views of outer space. For example, there might be only two disks, one white and the other black, arranged on either side of a horizon line to suggest the sun and moon passing around the earth.

Sandy packed up his circus and returned to New York in December 1930. The chief reason for this trip was that he and Louisa James had decided to marry. They had been corresponding for some time, finally concluding that they wanted to live together. The wedding was scheduled to take place in mid-January in Louisa's hometown, Concord, Massachusetts. Sandy lugged his trunks of circus paraphernalia to Concord and, on the night before the wedding, presented a performance at the James home. It was certainly an original way to celebrate the eve of one's marriage! The stuffier members of the James family and some of their friends must have been more than a little startled by the pudgy-faced, curly-haired "wire sculptor," who blew whistles, made animal sounds and played with toy chariots. What ominous thoughts must have passed through the mind of Louisa's father!

Sandy thought it would be a nice gesture to give Louisa a "homemade" wedding ring. With the help of a Paris jeweler, Sandy designed a gold ring with a spiral on top. But he hadn't taken Louisa's ideas into account. She persistently referred to the ring as her "engagement" ring and made it clear that she expected a more conventional wedding band. Sandy finally gave in, but since he was never a big spender, he bought a two-dollar ring. Louisa eventually came to prefer Sandy's handcrafted ring to the cheap, store-bought wedding band. The "engagement" ring became the forerunner of dozens of pieces of jewelry that Calder made for her over the years.

A few days after their marriage, Sandy and Louisa sailed for Europe and set up house in his Paris apartment in Villa Brune. One of the first things Louisa had to get used to was the maze of wires and strings in the place. Calder had rigged all the door latches with string. He could sit in the bathtub and, by pulling a string, open the front door. There was a more elaborate contraption for carrying the morning coffee to the bed. By pulling on one string, he lit the gas under the percolator; another string turned the gas off. The coffeepot itself was conveyed to the bed on a sort of cradle, suspended from two wires. If the device failed, Sandy got out of bed, fixed it, returned to bed and resumed the whole operation.

While abstract painting presented Calder with insoluble problems, abstract sculpture did not; and he began to have more success with his art. It was easy for him to think in terms of wire. His experience at modeling three-dimensional figures of people and animals in wire had provided him with exceptional skill in defining spatial relations with a minimum of lines. By twisting and bending wire, he now was able to compose satisfying abstract shapes that eluded him on canvas. In eliminating the representational element, he concentrated on simple abstract shapes—circles, arcs and angled lines.

Sandy had become friendly with several artists who belonged to an association with the imposing name "Abstraction-Création," which was dedicated to advancing the cause of abstract art. The artists invited Sandy to join their group, then helped him get a show of his abstract sculpture at the Galerie Percier. The brochure to the exhibition, which opened in April 1931, was rather cryptic, announcing: "Volumes–Vectors–Densities–Drawings–Portraits." Sandy felt apologetic about including the wire portraits because they were figurative and, therefore, not as "modern" as the remainder of the show. But the portraits of his friends, which he had been making since about 1928, were too good to leave out; so he hung them in a row, high on the walls. One of the most striking was of the widely known French painter Fernand Léger, whom Calder caricatured by emphasizing his bushy eyebrows, large nose and jutting chin. When subjected to a breeze, the wire portraits vibrated ever so slightly, making them nearly as animated as real faces.

The abstract constructions were displayed on makeshift pedestals—wooden planks, painted white, that were balanced on top of empty champagne crates. Many of the constructions were extremely spare—almost skimpy—in form, consisting of just a few pieces of wire and one or two wooden balls. The wire was most frequently bent into simple geometric figures. By joining two wire circles, one horizontal and the other vertical, Calder created a sphere in the most economical way. The two intersecting hoops of wire reminded him not only of a sphere, but also of the solar system itself, so he titled many of them "Universe." In some constructions, he attached a small wooden ball to one end of a piece of wire, then fastened the other end of the wire to the rest of the sculpture so that the wooden ball hovered like a tiny satellite outside the main body of the work. Several of the pieces looked like scale models of imaginary universes.

Twenty years later, Calder, in one of his rare attempts to explain his art, wrote: "The underlying sense of form in my work has been the system of the universe." He conceded (in one of his major understatements) that the universe was "a rather large model to work from." But he maintained that "the idea of detached bodies floating in space, of different sizes and densities, perhaps of different colors and temperatures, surrounded and interlarded with wisps of gaseous condition, and some at rest, while others move in peculiar manners, seems to me the ideal source of form."

In this first show of his abstract art, Calder's sculpture displayed two characteristics that would appear constantly in his future work: intentional references to the solar system and a pronounced taste for curved forms. He probably felt that curved lines were more graceful than straight lines, and more in keeping with the nature of the cosmos. In this respect he differed from Mondrian, who spurned curves and used only straight edges and right angles in his work.

During the spring of 1931, Sandy and Louisa gave up the cramped apartment in Villa Brune and rented a furnished, three-story house with a top-floor studio on the Rue de la Colonie, located on Paris's Left Bank. Louisa, ever ready to avoid

Up, Over the Horizon, 1931. Ink drawing, 19⅝" x 25½". Collection Joseph H. Hirshhorn.

Calder's early ventures in abstraction resemble views of outer space.

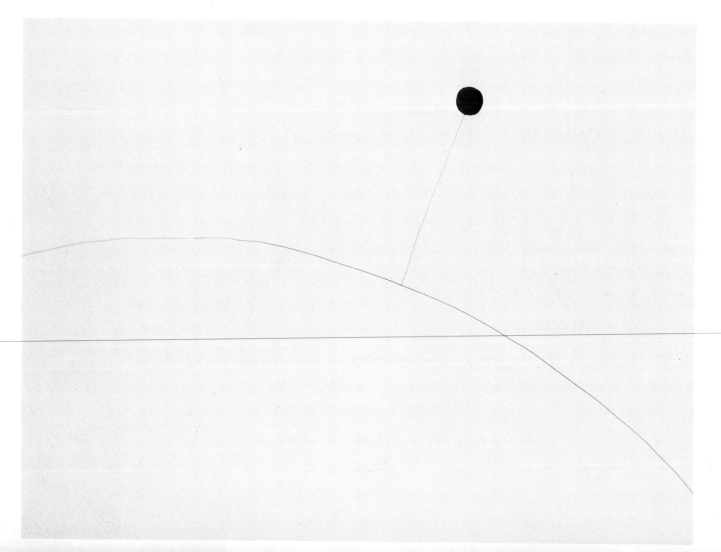

the drudgery of housekeeping, acquired a piano and induced Sandy to hire a maid. But the most beloved addition to their household at this time was a fox-terrier puppy which they named Feathers. For years to come, Feathers accompanied them nearly everywhere.

After they decided to hire a cook, Louisa went out to buy a pitcher and washbasin. Sandy expected her to return with a type of French jug known as a *broc.* "Now, a *broc* is a beautiful thing of conical shape, tall and slender—and instead she had bought a pitcher, fat and dumpy," he complained.

"You won't see these things anyway," Louisa told him, "because they'll be in the cook's room."

But Sandy was so enraged that he took the pitcher and washbasin and spitefully drove spikes through them. "I feel that if one accepts things which one does not approve of," he explained, "it is the beginning of the end, and by and by you get more things of a similar nature. This is akin to the stunt of giving objects away which you don't like. Then the people think you do like that sort of thing, and pretty soon they'll

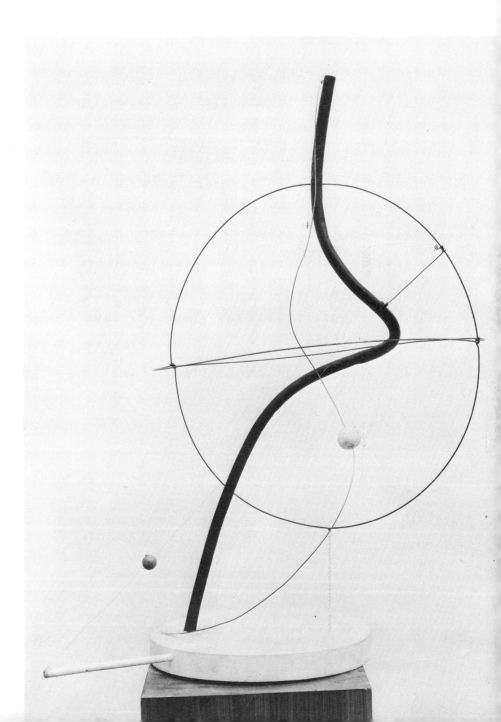

A Universe, 1934. Motorized mobile: painted iron pipe, wire and wood with string, 40½" h. The Museum of Modern Art, New York; gift of Abby Aldrich Rockefeller.

"The underlying sense of form in my work has been the system of the universe."

give you back something of a similar nature. Bad taste always boomerangs."

Sandy and Louisa entertained a lot on Rue de la Colonie, playing host to nearly the entire membership of Abstraction-Création, which included Mondrian. Calder and Mondrian were an unlikely pair of friends, but they did share several things in common. Both adored Paris, and Mondrian was zealous in his praise of French cooking. Mondrian regularly attended the cafés and music halls and, like Calder, was a fan of the Fratellini brothers and an enthusiastic admirer of Josephine Baker. When it came to dancing, Mondrian was perhaps even more fanatic than Calder; Mondrian's specialties were the fox-trot and tango. Sandy and Louisa assembled a large record collection, and Mondrian became its most severe critic. When visiting, he listened intently to their phonograph, nodding or shaking his head, and declaring: "That's good," or "That's no good."

Sandy's carefree existence was threatened when he learned that Stirling, back in New York, was finishing a major project. For some time, Stirling had been working on one of his most important commissions, a monumental statue of Leif Ericsson, the Norse hero who may have discovered America around A.D. 1000. The sculpture had been commissioned by the United States government as a gift to Iceland in commemoration of the one-thousandth anniversary of the Icelandic parliament. Stirling's ten-foot-high statue was designed to stand on a granite pedestal, placed on a hill overlooking the city of Reykjavik. Stirling wanted Sandy to go to Reykjavik to supervise the installation.

Sandy did not relish the prospect of going to Iceland, and he felt embarrassed by his predicament. He did not want to refuse his father's request, but neither did he want to risk the ridicule of his Paris friends. His father's monumental work typified the kind of romantic, storytelling statuary that the Abstraction-Création group held in disdain.

At this particular point, the two Calders, father and son, exemplified the polarities of American sculpture. Stirling represented the academic "old guard," which was rapidly going out of fashion. His heroic, romantic realism was intended to induce rousing, ennobling spirits in the spectator; but the style was no longer expressive of the times. Sandy's abstract wire constructions represented the new, experimental attitude.

Luckily, Stirling changed his mind and decided not to ask Sandy to go to Iceland. Feeling greatly relieved, Sandy and Louisa left Feathers with friends, and vacationed on Majorca, an island off the coast of Spain.

DURING THE TIME THEY LIVED IN PARIS, Sandy and Louisa befriended several Americans, including Mary Reynolds. She visited them one night during the winter of 1931-32, bringing along her close companion, the French artist Marcel Duchamp. This was the same Duchamp who had achieved notoriety in the 1913 Armory Show with his painting of a nude woman descending a staircase. He hadn't painted anything in years and his reputation had faded. But he continued to be keenly interested in what the younger artists were doing.

Sandy showed his abstract constructions to Duchamp, who examined them thoughtfully. Since Calder was developing rapidly as an artist, his work seemed to be proceeding in many directions. His wire "universes" had been motionless, but it occurred to him soon after that he could equip the wire constructions with motors, gears and cranks, in order to make the various elements actually move. At first the movements were not very complicated. But Sandy, drawing upon his engineering background, gradually progressed to more ambitious movements, with the elements being driven in different directions at varied tempos.

Duchamp was particularly intrigued by one of Sandy's new motor-driven constructions. Reaching toward it, Duchamp asked, "Do you mind?"

Sandy had just finished painting the piece but, before he could warn his visitor, Duchamp gave it a shove—getting wet paint on his hands. It was an embarrassing moment; but Sandy, in later years, would gleefully retell the story.

One reason Duchamp expressed interest in Sandy's work was that the French artist had experimented with motion at a much earlier date, and perhaps saw the Calder constructions as a belated vindication of his pioneering endeavors in this area. In 1913, Duchamp had devised a moving construction that is probably the first "mobile" sculpture of the twentieth century. It consisted of a bicycle wheel, turned upside down and affixed to an ordinary kitchen stool which he painted white (page 56). Anyone who happened to be nearby could set the wheel spinning—and at any speed, since it took only another touch of the hand to accelerate or slow the wheel. By mounting the bicycle wheel upside down, Duchamp deprived it of its original function and turned it into an object for contemplation. "To see that wheel turning was very soothing, very comforting," Duchamp recalled.

Sandy, unfamiliar with a great deal of modern art, possibly did not know about Duchamp's bicycle wheel or his ambitious contraption of 1920, "Rotary Glass Plates"—a motorized, freestanding construction with five painted-glass plates

that revolved when the motor was turned on. But Sandy was surely acquainted with some of the numerous artistic experiments with movement that were being conducted all over Europe. It is conceivable, of course, that Sandy gathered information and advice from other artists in the Abstraction-Création circle. In any case, as Duchamp himself remarked, "The whole idea of movement, of speed, was in the air."

Sandy and Duchamp discussed what sort of name might be given to this type of work, and the Frenchman promptly suggested the word "mobile." In English, the word was almost always used as an adjective, signifying something movable or changeable. From then on, the word "mobile" also served as a noun, defined in one dictionary as: "a construction or sculpture frequently of wire and sheet metal shapes with parts that can be set in motion by air currents."

Duchamp not only provided the name for

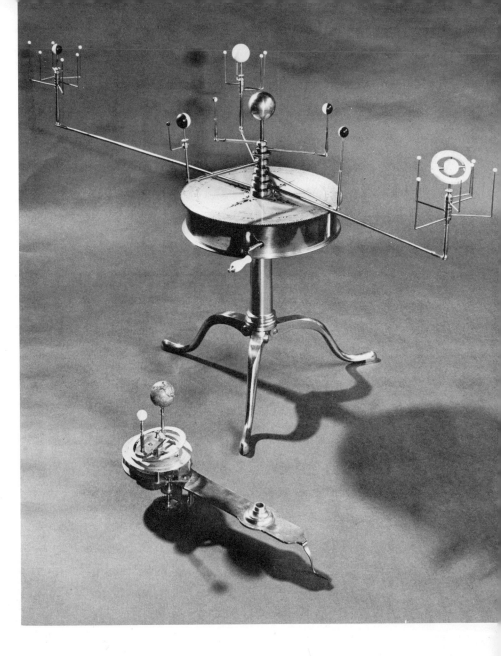

OPPOSITE: Sandy, assembling a mobile, *Nine Discs*, outside his home in Roxbury, Connecticut in 1937.
RIGHT: Orrery on a brass tripod stand, made by George Adams, Jr., c. 1790. Harriet Wynter Arts & Sciences, London.

Calder's early "space" drawings and constructions, with their deliberate references to the solar system, sometimes resemble an orrery, a scale model of the solar system with orbiting spheres representing the planets.

Calder's most celebrated works, but he also arranged for Sandy to show his new pieces at the Galerie Vignon in Paris. Calder's first show of mobiles, which opened at Galerie Vignon in February 1932, included fifteen objects with motors and about fifteen others without motors, but with moving elements that could be set in motion by string or gears. Sandy labored almost nonstop to produce enough works for the show and, on opening day, worked right up to the last minute—greasing and adjusting the gears of his mobiles until they ran properly.

Nearly all of Sandy's friends in the Abstrac-

LEFT: Marcel Duchamp, *Bicycle Wheel*, 1951 (third version, after lost original of 1913). Assemblage: metal wheel mounted on painted wood stool, overall 50½" h. The Museum of Modern Art, New York; the Sidney and Harriet Janis Collection.

Duchamp, who provided Calder with the term "mobile," was also a pioneer of moving sculpture. For Duchamp, the sight of the spinning wheel was "very soothing, very comforting. . . ."

OPPOSITE: Folk sculpture, *The Sport World*, c. 1910. Whirligig-vane: painted wood with iron, gesso and shingles, 90" l. Made near Gap, Pennsylvania. Collection Michael and Julie Hall.

Whirligigs, part weather vane and part toy, were among the animated objects that intrigued Calder. This whirligig's propellers indicate velocity while activating human figures who ride seesaws and a type of merry-go-round.

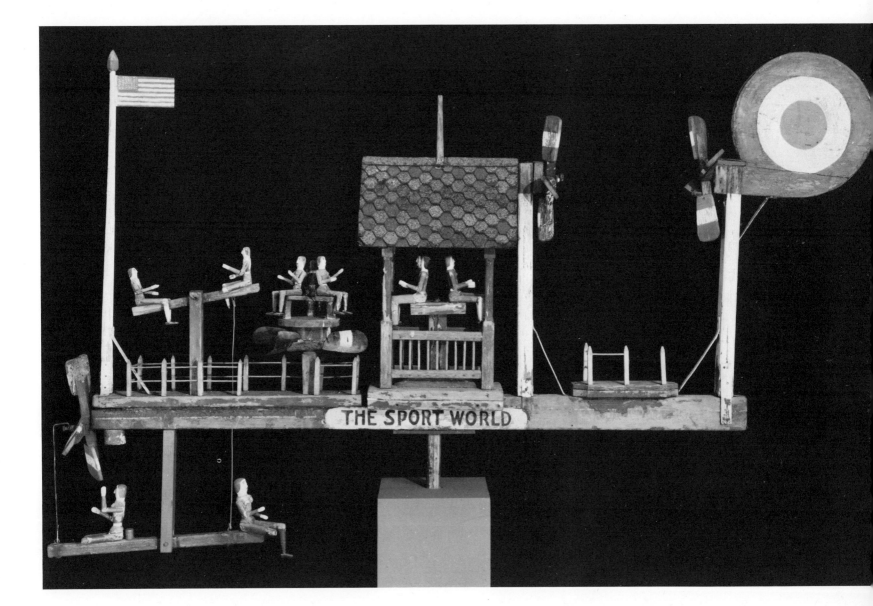

tion-Création group showed up. One of them, the sculptor Jean Arp, took one look at the mobiles and wisecracked, "Well, if these are mobiles, what do you call those things you had in the show last year—were they stabiles?" The word "stabile" struck Sandy as a good name for his stationary sculptures; so he adopted that word, too, applying it to most of his non-moving sculpture. Like the noun "mobile," "stabile" also found its way into dictionaries, where it is defined as: "a stable abstract sculpture or construction typically made of sheet metal, wire, and wood."

The mobiles were reviewed favorably in one of the Paris newspapers by the American writer Waverley Root, who observed that time was an essential ingredient both to their existence, and their perception. "Calder's mobiles may well be the beginning of four-dimensional sculpture," Root wrote. It takes time, obviously, to look at any piece of sculpture. While the overall shape of a mobile can be glimpsed in a moment, it takes a certain amount of time to witness all the changes of which it is capable. Since time is generally considered to be as important a dimension as height, depth and width, Calder's mobiles are truly four-dimensional.

Sandy and Louisa remained in Europe for more than a year before deciding it was time for a visit home. In the spring of 1932, they lent their house to a friend, packed the circus trunks, gathered up the mobiles, stabiles and Feathers, and boarded a freighter. In New York, Sandy soon talked himself into a show with Julien Levy, a dealer who specialized in avant-garde art. The show, which opened in mid-May, featured several motor-driven mobiles.

Levy instantly regretted the show. Much to his annoyance, he realized that holes had to be gouged in the gallery walls to install new electrical outlets and, worse, that Sandy's electric motors blew fuses. Levy was equally disenchanted by the "repetitive, mechanical" quality of the motor-driven works. "I was furious," Levy recalled many years later, "and no doubt, unduly sarcastic, and when the time came for another show, to present the new and beautifully balanced mobiles for which he [Sandy] became famous, he turned to another dealer, Pierre Matisse."

Sandy's father attended the opening and was somewhat bewildered by the constructions. He became fascinated by a pulley that repeatedly drove an object around, and said it reminded him of a man on a motorcycle driving laps. "He was at least puzzled by what I made," Sandy gloated.

Stirling Calder felt uncomfortable amid the purring motors, throbbing wires and dancing balls. But when asked what he thought of his son's work, he sighed: "Well, we should always keep moving in a world so full of wonders."

Edward Alden Jewell, the art critic of *The New York Times,* declared that the mobiles were "something absolutely new in sculpture." He wrote that other artists "have long sought to persuade the world that motion in art should be actually rather than statically dynamic." Calder, he noted approvingly, "has startled Paris with abstractions that, whatever skepticism may attend the net result, really do work!"

Henry McBride, the art critic of the *New York Sun,* was less enchanted.

In spite of the fact that this sculpture looks like machinery and moves like machinery, it is scarcely the sort of thing that we Americans would be likely to encourage. It needed the dark, dull afternoons of a Paris winter for its inception, and needed them also, once the work has been finished, for its appreciation. . . . At any rate we can be fascinated at once by the cute little motors that run these discs and wires and small planets. They are no bigger than your fist. And the Saturns and Jupiters, if that is what they are, [that] move so lazily on their orbits, that, too, is fun. . . . "Slight," will be the hard-boiled, native art-appraiser's comment on this, "very slight"; and possibly in the final analysis young Calder's work may turn out to be so. As for young Mr. Calder, we don't have to do anything in particular for him, since Paris has quite adopted him. . . .

McBride seemed resentful of Calder's modest success in Paris, insinuating that the mobiles were too frivolous to be taken seriously in America. It is ironic that Calder should have been disowned simultaneously by two nations. The French viewed him as typically American, brimming with Yankee ingenuity and mechanical know-how. Fernand Léger, in writing the preface to the show of stabiles at Galerie Percier in 1931, declared that Calder was "100 percent American." To Americans, however, Calder's work appeared too Frenchified; that is—precious, affected, and, as McBride put it, "scarcely the sort of thing that we Americans would be likely to encourage." Although Calder's work would play an increasingly significant role in the history of both French and American art, it did not seem, in the early 1930s, to conform to either country's image of itself.

However, Calder went right on tinkering with his mobiles until he launched himself into the international mainstream of art, becoming one of the great masters of modern sculpture.

Calder's mobiles represent only a fraction of his total output, but they reveal a surprisingly diverse range of physical and expressive qualities. Some mobiles are motorized, while others are propelled by air currents. Some mobiles are freestanding constructions, while many hang from the ceiling. In size, they range from a few inches to more than fifty feet. Some mobiles have an essentially vertical configuration while others are basically horizontal. In their rhythmic

patterns, they range from the flighty and easily agitated to the languorous and stately. Calder's mobiles, in short, come in all sizes, shapes and tempos.

One of the best examples of a motor-driven mobile is "A Universe" (page 51), made in 1934. This construction has two wire circles intersecting in such a way as to create the volume of a sphere. A curved piece of iron pipe, fastened to the base of the piece, rises upward through the sphere. In addition, there are two lengths of wire: one S-shaped wire rises from the base to the top of the iron pipe; the second wire is straight and runs diagonally from a rod inserted in the base to the upper part of the wire sphere. Each wire is strung through a small ball. When the motor is turned on, the wires vibrate, causing the balls to move up and down—usually at different speeds and in different directions. The movement suggests two tiny satellites moving through and around a large, stationary body.

The motor-driven mobiles were important to

Lobster Trap and Fish Tail, 1939. Hanging mobile: painted steel wire and sheet aluminum, approx. 8'6" x 9'6". The Museum of Modern Art, New York; commissioned by the Advisory Committee for the stairwell of the museum.
One of the most graceful and sophisticated of the early mobiles, this piece evokes an underwater world; metal blades shaped like fins and tails float languorously around a wire basket similar to those used for capturing lobsters.

Calder's development because they enabled him to experiment with various kinds of movement. But they presented two big problems. The first problem was the repetitive, predictable patterns that result from mechanization. Sandy attempted to make his motor-driven mobiles less predictable by imposing relatively random patterns of movement. He felt he could achieve more interesting effects if he combined two or more simple movements with contrasting rhythms and rates of speed. But the process was difficult, and he was seldom pleased with the results. The second problem was that it was extremely laborious to make all the necessary gears. The motors, he complained, were "too much bother—they always needed fixing." So he looked for a way to make the mobiles simpler to operate.

It then occurred to Sandy that the movement of his mobiles would be relatively free, capable of many more variations, if they were propelled by currents of air, instead of electric motors. By the mid-thirties he was making wind-driven mobiles that dangle from the ceiling. For thousands of years, sculpture had been oriented to the earth, and it seemed a radical and startling idea to hang sculpture from the ceiling. The mobile had no base or pedestal in any conventional sense and, while it was still subject to gravity, it was easily stirred by air currents.

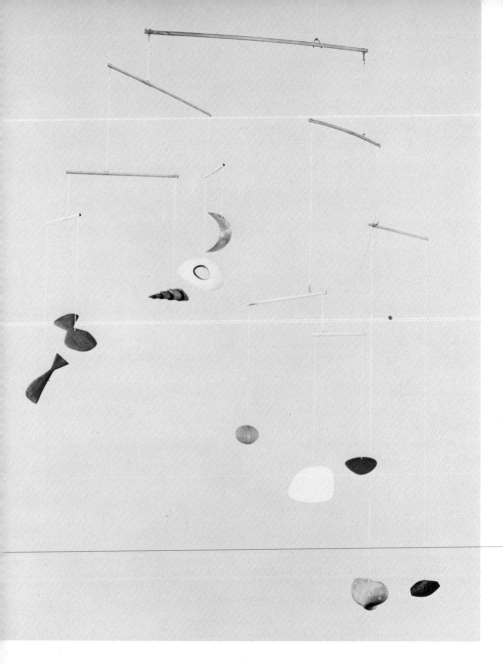

The movements of a hanging mobile are completely spontaneous and unpredictable, depending only on the circulation of the air. Often, one cluster or set of elements revolves more quickly than the overall piece, which may rotate at a more leisurely pace. Most spectators, if confronted with a passive mobile, are tempted to give it a nudge, setting it in motion. Calder never minded if the mobiles were given a gentle send-off by hand, but he became angry at anyone who shoved or swatted a mobile, causing it to spin or bob wildly.

"Snow Flurry I" (page 5), which Calder made in 1948, is considerably more complex and sophisticated than the earlier mobiles of the mid-thirties. As the title indicates, this mobile with its thirty-one white disks could represent a sparkling dance of snowflakes, flying this way and that, as propelled by gusts of wind. Like the earlier hanging mobile, this one has its elements arranged vertically in tiers. But, instead of cord, Calder used a set of curved wires, each ending with a disk. Where the pieces of cord in the ear-

Untitled, c. 1943–46. Hanging mobile: wood, metal, cord, approx. 67" h. The Solomon R. Guggenheim Museum, New York; Mary Reynolds Collection, gift of her brother.

The tin crescent is the only piece of metal in this mobile, made during the war years when metal was scarce. The other elements are carved and painted wood, all suspended from wood dowels.

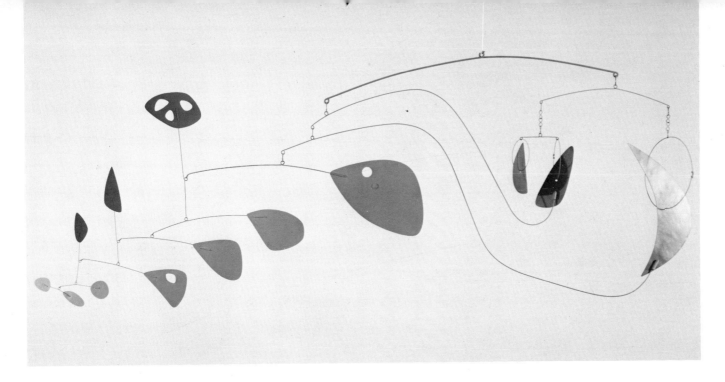

lier mobile merely hung straight down, the much stronger wires are capable of branching sideways and upwards in graceful configurations.

Part of the appeal of Calder's mobiles is that they seemingly mimic things in the real world. Mobiles frequently remind people of various types of movement that exist in everyday life, from such natural phenomena as snow flurries and tree branches swaying in the wind, to an almost animal kind of activity, such as a school of fish or flock of birds abruptly changing direction. In fact, many mobiles occasionally *behave* like living things, in the sense that they conduct

Three Gongs and Red, c. 1953. Hanging mobile: metal, 28" x 68". Collection Mr. and Mrs. Klaus G. Perls, New York.

One of several "musical" mobiles, this work has two tiny steel knobs that randomly strike the three brass fins at right.

themselves according to certain patterns and rhythms. Unlike a machine, which repeats the same purposeful motions over and over, a wind-driven mobile can be downright whimsical. It seemingly moves according to its own personality and temperament.

Calder made one of his largest mobiles, forty-

five feet in diameter, in 1958 for Kennedy International Airport in New York, where it dominated the ceiling of the International Arrival Lobby. Its title, ".125," derives from the thickness of its steel plate (.125 inch) which was cut out in leaflike shapes. ".125" proves that the mobile, as a structural form, has almost limitless possibilities, and that the concept is equally valid for both minute and monumental constructions.

Calder's mobiles, especially those that hang from the ceiling, seem to symbolize the interest in air and flight that characterizes the early twentieth century—a period that has been called both the "air age" and the "machine age." Obviously, mobiles are not as technically complicated as airplanes and rockets, but they tell us something about the age's preoccupation with aeronautics, mechanical engineering, even automation. In the early part of the century aviation was still in its youth, spaceships existed only in science fiction, and most people firmly believed that industrial mechanization could lead only to a

Red Flock, c. 1949. Hanging mobile: metal, 34" x 65". The Phillips Collection, Washington, D.C.

Untitled, 1977. Hanging mobile: honeycomb aluminum and steel, 70' w. National Gallery of Art, Washington, D.C.
This mammoth mobile, designed specifically for the vast central court of the National Gallery's East Building, was completed and installed after Calder's death in 1976.

better world. The face of the Earth had been pretty well explored during the nineteenth century, and people now aspired to conquer air and space, whether in airplanes or through the construction of skyscrapers of unprecedented height. Humankind's most exciting adventures were taking place in the air, and Calder's mobiles expressed that adventure as did no other sculpture.

65

7 THE EARLY 1930s were an especially happy time in Calder's life. All his interests and ambitions seemed to be coming into focus. He had found new happiness in his personal life, and his invention of the mobile had given direction and momentum to his career. Almost alone among the American artists of his generation, he had won the friendship and moral support of such avant-garde artists as Mondrian, Duchamp and Léger, all of whom encouraged Calder to stick with abstract art.

Sandy and Louisa enjoyed their summer-long stay in the United States, but were eager to get back to Paris. In the fall, they packed the circus trunks, gathered up Feathers and departed for Europe. Because of the Depression, which in 1932 had not yet bottomed out, they traveled cheaply on a Spanish ship that took fourteen days to cross the Atlantic to Spain.

Sandy and Louisa disembarked in Barcelona, then boarded a train that, within a few hours, brought them to the village of Montroig. Their chief motive in stopping off in Spain was to pay a visit to Joan Miró, an artist whom Calder had known in Paris. Miró customarily spent his winters in Paris, his summers on his mother's farm in Montroig.

The Calders were happy to find Miró in Montroig and they settled in for a week-long stay. A short, rather stocky man, Miró had a handsome face with darkly poetic eyes and thin lips. He seldom spoke and was, in fact, noted for his long silences. Language was not the problem—even though the Calders communicated with Miró in French. Louisa, whose French was stilted, could hardly conceal her irritation. She found it maddening that all Miró ever seemed to say was "Comment ça va? Ca va?" which translates roughly as, "How are things? All right?"

Miró, who was five years older than Calder, had settled in Paris in 1920, and by the mid-twenties had won acclaim as one of the major artists of the surrealist movement. He had won this reputation with works like "The Harlequin's Carnival" (page 68). Miró's carnival is confined to the interior of a room, swarming with fanciful creatures. Every portion of the picture is filled with agitated beings and curious objects, frequently of the most preposterous appearance. Harlequin himself is a round-faced man whose mustache extends upward on one side, downward on the other.

Of all the artists who were to play a crucial role in Calder's development, Miró was the one to exert the most sustained influence. Mondrian had opened Calder's eyes to abstraction, and Duchamp had encouraged Calder to make mov-

66

ing sculpture. Miró's influence, however, was more profound—though it took Calder several years to realize it.

Although he took a personal liking to Miró at their very first meeting, in Paris during the winter of 1928–29, Calder at first did not see much merit in the Spaniard's work. Miró, who then kept a studio in Montmartre, showed Calder some of the things he had been making, including a sheet of cardboard embellished with a feather, a cork and a picture postcard. Calder was frankly puzzled. "It did not look like art to me," he said.

Eventually, Calder came to admire Miró's art and was gradually influenced by the Spaniard's inventive, organic-looking shapes. Miró's forms —curlicues, spirals, asterisks, blobs and crescents—look as if they are based on things in nature, no matter how far removed from realistic representation. The surfaces of Miró's canvases are punctuated by symbols or ideograms—an astonishing array of cryptic, shorthand representations of stars, moons, people and fantastic animals.

Calder, like Miró, had little inclination toward "pure" abstraction. Instead, they found their inspiration in the natural world. They were as filled with wonder by such distant phenomena as constellations and moons, as they were en-

tranced by the unpredictable antics of cats, dogs and cows. Hardly anything in the visible world was too vast or too humble to escape their attention. In addition they shared an earthy and often whimsical sense of humor.

During his stay in Montroig, Calder presented a circus performance before Miró, his wife, Pilar, their daughter and a gathering of farmhands and neighbors. It was a festive occasion, accompanied by red wine. Afterward, Miró told Calder he liked best the bits of weighted paper—the "doves"—that fluttered downward on wires to the shoulders of the prima donna.

Miró believed in keeping himself physically fit. One day he managed to talk Sandy into joining him in outdoor exercise. Miró proceeded to breathe in air through his nose and exhale through the mouth with such great whistling noises that Sandy was reduced to fits of laughter.

On the day Sandy and Louisa were to board the train to Barcelona, the car that Miró had hired did not arrive in time. Sandy heard a whistle as their train pulled into the station, then another whistle as the train departed. The car finally arrived a half-hour later. Sandy, Louisa, Miró and Feathers scrambled into the car and sped to the station, knowing they had no chance of catching their train. There was nothing to do

but wait for the next train, which meant sitting in the station with Miró for three silent hours.

Calder had more than enough projects to keep himself occupied during the early months of 1933. In February, he returned to Spain to present circus performances in Madrid and Barcelona. In Paris that spring he was one of six artists included in a group show at Pierre Loeb's gallery. The other artists were Miró, Arp, the

OPPOSITE: Joan Miró. *The Harlequin's Carnival,* 1924–25. Oil painting, 26″ x 36⅝″. Albright-Knox Art Gallery, Buffalo, New York; Room of Contemporary Art Fund.

A menagerie of bizarre creatures and a circuslike atmosphere spread throughout this startling picture, filled with incongruous, surrealistic elements such as disembodied eyes and a human ear that sprouts from a ladder. Harlequin, smoking a long pipe, stands in the left half of the picture, midway between the ladder and the female guitarplayer. A pair of relatively realistic cats play with string in the right foreground.

ABOVE: *Turquoise.* Handmade mat of manila hemp, 5′ x 7′. CAC Publications, New York.

Calder's organic forms correspond to those in the art of Miró and Arp.

RIGHT: Jean Arp. *Constellation in Five White Forms and Two Black, Variation III,* 1932. Relief: oil on wood, 23⅝″ x 29⅝″. Solomon R. Guggenheim Museum, New York.

Arp derived his abstract forms from nature. The shapes in this relief resemble simple one-celled organisms like those found in the phylum Protozoa.

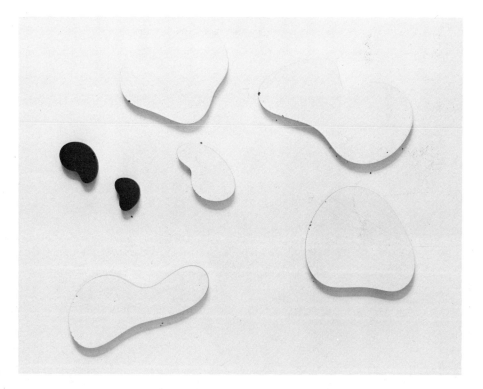

French abstract painter Jean Hélion, the Russian-born constructivist sculptor Antoine Pevsner and the surrealist painter Kurt Seligmann. Calder became upset one day when he entered the gallery and found Loeb and some of his visitors merrily bouncing one of his mobiles. They were throwing all the elements of the mobile into the air at once, Calder complained, damaging the bars and ruining the movement.

In May, Calder had a one-man exhibition at the Pierre Colle Galerie. The show was favorably reviewed in a magazine titled *Mouvement*:

Some of Calder's compositions are filled with celestial conjunctions, and other coincidences, which can be observed as the eye becomes aware of the recurrent cycles of movement. In one case there are two simple sticks, one white and one black, which are driven by a hidden motor that buzzes like a hive. . . . The sticks vibrate, rise up, almost meet, then fall away from each other, with the grace, uncertainty and timidity of rudimentary, schematic beings. The observer is mesmerized by them.

In June 1933, Sandy and Louisa gave up the lease on their Paris house and returned to the United States. Their first destination was Concord, Massachusetts, where they visited Louisa's parents. In Concord they purchased a secondhand 1930 La Salle touring car. It had a removable cloth top and could seat as many as nine people; also, it was roomy enough to transport Calder's work. Eventually, they drove off in the La Salle to Richmond, Massachusetts, to visit Sandy's parents.

Afterward, Sandy and Louisa began to scout for a house of their own. Calder wanted a modest country house, preferably one with a barn that he could convert into a studio. They househunted along the Housatonic River from western Connecticut to Long Island Sound. They explored Westchester and Rockland counties in New York; in Connecticut, they looked around Westport and Danbury. In Roxbury, Connecticut, a real-estate agent led them to Painter Hill Road where, from the top of a hill, they saw a two-story house with a pitched roof. Both Sandy and Louisa exclaimed: "That's it!"

Only one thing was missing: the barn. Two years earlier it had been struck by lightning and had burned to its foundations.

They bought the house and eighteen acres of land for $3,500, a sum that sounds absurdly low today, but was the going price for land during the worst years of the Depression. Although the house was in need of many repairs, and the rolling acreage was overgrown with weeds, Sandy and Louisa felt elated about owning a home of their own. Feathers, of course, was ecstatic; for him, it was like having the dog's equivalent of a feudal estate. The property included an old icehouse that was dug into the ground on two sides. Sandy got some secondhand windows, stuck them into the two wooden walls, and turned the former icehouse into a space where he could work. It was the first time he had a studio separate from his living quarters.

During August, Calder's work was included in a group show of modern painting and sculpture at the Berkshire Museum in Pittsfield, Massachusetts. For this occasion, he wrote one of his rare catalog statements, in which he inquired: "Why not plastic forms in motion? . . . Just as one can compose colors, or forms, so one can compose motions." He went on to explain: "The two motor-driven 'mobiles' which I am exhibiting are from among the most successful of my earliest attempts at plastic objects in motion." Both mobiles were acquired for the museum.

In April 1934, Calder had a one-man exhibition of mobiles at the Pierre Matisse Gallery in New York. Matisse was chiefly interested in School of Paris painters, such as Raoul Dufy, Georges Rouault, and Miro—whose paintings the Matisse Gallery had exhibited during the winter. But Calder seemed to fit in with Matisse's stable of artists and, over the next several years, the American had many one-man shows at the gallery.

Little Spider, c. 1940. Standing mobile: painted sheet metal, rod and wire, 55" x 40". Collection Mr. and Mrs. Klaus G. Perls, New York.

During the previous year in Paris, Sandy had met the American art critic James Johnson Sweeney, a great champion of Miró's work. Sandy decided to ask Sweeney to write a preface for the brochure that would accompany the first Calder show at the Matisse Gallery. Sweeney responded with a brief but eloquent statement in which he claimed that "Calder's work epitomizes the evolution of plastic art in the present century."

Sandy was disappointed when only a few friends attended the opening of his show. Throughout the exhibition, he hung around the gallery, zealously explaining his work to spectators. At Sandy's urging, the president of his old school, Stevens Institute, paid a visit. Unfortunately, Sandy missed him and later felt compelled to send the man an explanatory letter. The president of Stevens Institute never acknowledged the letter, which Calder took as "proof" that the school was not interested in his career.

Louisa was pregnant and, during the following winter, moved in with her parents in Concord. She wanted to have her baby amid tranquil surroundings. Sandy continued to live in Roxbury, but frequently visited Concord, usually bringing Louisa a gift of flowers. Once he brought Louisa a mobile made with mirrors, tilted in such a way that they reflected the sun onto the ceiling but the

dots of light darting about on the ceiling bothered her, and Louisa demanded the mobile's immediate removal.

During her pregnancy, Louisa had learned chess. She and Sandy were in the middle of a chess game one April evening in 1935, when she abruptly announced: "Let's go to the hospital." Before the night was out, she had given birth to a daughter. For more than two weeks Louisa convalesced in the hospital and debated with Sandy what to call their child. They finally settled on the name Sandra, the feminine diminutive of Alexander.

In 1935, Sandy received his first theatrical commission. Martha Graham, a pioneer of modern dance, asked him to design mobiles for a production of her *Panorama* at the Bennington School of Dance in Vermont. Sandy arrived on campus in his La Salle, accompanied by Feathers. According to Martha Graham's manager, Frances Hawkins, "Sandy was wearing a shirt with the sleeves torn out, bedroom slippers with purple pompoms on them and no pants—only undershorts. I was asked if I would take him into town to get some proper clothes, and we located a clothing store in the then small village. Sandy said to the storekeeper, 'I need a pair of pants.' The storekeeper, a typical Vermonter, looked Sandy up and down and said, 'You sure do.'"

72

The following year, Sandy made the mobile settings for a production of Erik Satie's "symphonic drama" *Socrate* in Hartford, Connecticut. Though this musical work has no dancers, Calder's set provided a sort of abstract ballet. For the first nine minutes, a red disk about thirty inches in diameter moved continuously from side to side, pulled by cords. The second section featured two steel hoops, seven feet in diameter and joined at right angles to suggest a sphere; they rotated for a few minutes, moved toward the floor, rotated in the opposite direction, then moved upward. All the while a white, vertical rectangle, ten feet high, had been standing on the floor. In the third section, this door-shaped panel tilted gently over to one side until it rested on its long edge, than fell over slowly, away from the audience. It rose up again—showing its other face, which was black—stood upright and moved off.

"The whole thing," said Calder, "was very gentle, and subservient to the music and the words."

In May 1937, Sandy and Louisa, who had spent the winter in New York, set off to visit

Sandy, who liked to dance, taught some lively steps to Sandra as Louisa provided the music. Roxbury, Connecticut, 1937.

friends in Varengeville on the coast of Normandy in France. In addition to Sandra and Feathers, they now had so many circus trunks and pieces of luggage that it required two trips in the La Salle to transport all their belongings to the dock in New York. Because of so much luggage, they were the last ones off the boat when they arrived in France.

"Where do your things end?" the customs inspector wanted to know. "There?"

"No," Sandy said, "over there."

"There?" the customs man asked, pointing farther.

"No, over there."

The Calders spent only a few days in Varengeville before moving on to Paris, which they had not seen for four years. Calder looked up Miró and accompanied him one day to the site of the Paris International Exposition, where Miró was to paint a mural for the Spanish Pavilion. The pavilion was in a confused state, partly reflecting the political turmoil of Spain itself, which was in the midst of a civil war. The building was being constructed by the Loyalist government, which was under siege by Insurgent forces.

Spain's most famous living artist, Pablo Picasso, had also been asked to paint a mural for the Spanish Pavilion, but he whiled away several months without doing anything about it. Sud-

denly, in late April, he sprang into action, prodded by one of the most monstrous incidents of the war. The ancient town of Guernica, the center of Basque culture, had been obliterated in a single afternoon by bombers flying for the Insurgent forces. The bombardment of the defenseless town lasted more than three hours. Meanwhile, low-flying fighter planes, equipped with machine guns, strafed the fleeing civilians. Within six weeks, Picasso completed his famous mural, "Guernica," a powerful memorial to the innocent victims of war.

Miró responded less directly to the bloodshed in Spain by painting a mural called "The Reaper," a savage image of a man with a sickle, silhouetted against a sky with ominous-looking clouds. The following year his native city, Barcelona, would be subjected to daily aerial bombardment.

Excited by all the nervous energy and bustling activity in the Spanish Pavilion, Sandy offered to do "something or other" for the pavilion. José Luis Sert, one of the architects of the pavilion, asked Sandy what he thought of a mercury fountain that was being installed. Sandy frowned, indicating he thought it looked like a plain drinking fountain. Sert then asked Sandy whether he thought he could do better and Sandy nodded.

Sert assured his colleagues at the Spanish Pa-

74

vilion that Calder would produce something "striking and unique," and did all he could to help Sandy get the commission. A few days later, according to Sert, Sandy "requested some mercury for a demonstration model and was told that it would be much too expensive. Undaunted, Sandy made his model in wire and tin and used lead shot instead of mercury to prove that his machine would move. It did move and it was approved. On my way home to Montparnasse, I saw a small group of bystanders gathered on the sidewalks opposite the Café du Dôme. Curious to see what the attraction was, I joined them— only to find Sandy kneeling on the sidewalk demonstrating his moving mercury fountain!"

The initial purpose of the fountain was to dramatize the famous mercury mines of Almadén, one of the richest mercury-mining regions in the world. Mercury, the only metal that is in a liquid state at room temperature, does not need coaxing to become animated—breaking up into globules and reforming as a mass. It would have been unimaginative and dull to display this marvelous metal in a "plain drinking fountain," and Calder did nothing of the sort.

Instead, he designed a multi-level iron fountain, more than eight feet high. The mercury was led to the fountain through an underground tube, forced up another tube, then spewed onto an iron basin that was long, narrow and nearly horizontal. From there, the mercury trickled into a wider and deeper basin, then spilled onto a chute. As the mercury poured off the chute, it slammed against the lower end of a movable steel rod which was attached to another movable rod. The upper rod was nearly vertical, with a red disk at the lower end, and the word "Almadén"— spelled out in brass wire—on top. The impact of the mercury caused the two rods, the red disk and the word "Almadén" to weave about.

The "Mercury Fountain" was a tremendous success. One French writer declared it a "masterpiece." The fountain, he wrote, "allowed the mercury to flow slowly, to collect itself into a mass, to scatter, to roll from time to time in melting pearls, to play perpetually by itself, to the delight of the public."

The Calders spent most of the summer in Varengeville, where they rented a house. Sandy did not have to look far for companionship because the village was virtually a summer art colony. Miró was there, and so were the dealers Pierre Loeb and Pierre Matisse. It was a festive summer with plenty of amateur music and energetic dancing. Louisa played her accordion and the French painter Georges Braque contributed to the merriment by playing his concertina. Once more Sandy proved to be a formidable dancer, nearly breaking the foot of Matisse's wife, Teeny, who many years later married Marcel Duchamp.

Sandy and Louisa decided to spend the winter in London, where he presented several circus performances and had a one-man show of mobiles and jewelry at the Mayor Gallery. The exhibition attracted a number of notables, including the English sculptor Henry Moore. Calder's jewelry, praised as chic, sold briskly. Kenneth

A family frolic with Sandy, Louisa, Sandra and Feathers, Roxbury, Connecticut, 1937.

Clark, then director of London's National Gallery, bought a piece of jewelry for his wife and a mobile for himself.

The critics were enthralled by what they called Calder's "enchanting toys." Anthony Blunt, writing in *The Spectator,* said:

The Mayor Gallery should be visited not because it contains any great works of art, but because it has a series of toys of the greatest ingenuity . . . their movements are beautiful. The rhythmic swing of the flexible wires and the dancing of the balls are as complicated and as finely executed as the steps in any ballet.

The reviewer in *The New Statesman and Nation* wrote:

Calder's first London show is so gay, so bright, so unpretentious that we might be tempted to forget that we are looking at works of art and expect rather a sign above the doors saying "Toys for Christmas!"

It was, as he put it, "An enchanting show!"

SANDY AND LOUISA SPENT THE SPRING and summer of 1938 becoming reacquainted with their Connecticut neighbors. In the fall of that year, a museum in Springfield, Massachusetts, staged a retrospective show of Calder's work, including mobiles, stabiles, drawings and watercolors. This was an important honor for Calder, who was now forty years old, because it marked the first time any museum had expressed serious interest in his art. While a great many people enjoyed his whimsical sculptures, few believed that his "enchanting toys" amounted to much as works of art.

Calder drove back and forth in the La Salle to Springfield, where he delivered the show by installments. At the same time he was supervising the construction of a new studio on the old foundations of the burned-down barn. He wanted plenty of light, so he installed tall windows, twelve feet high, along two walls. Because the two windows were fifteen and thirty feet wide, the studio came to resemble a greenhouse. As the building reached completion, Calder asked the carpenters to install about 150 screw eyes in the ceiling. These enabled him to suspend his mobiles at any height. Whenever he wanted to construct a mobile, he took a long stick with a wire hook at the end and attached a pulley to one of the screw eyes. The pulleys and ropes allowed him to work at whatever level he wished.

The new studio, which measured twenty-five by forty-five feet, at first appeared huge and uncluttered. But it was not long before it was crammed with various materials, tools, and finished mobiles which tinkled like wind chimes whenever a breeze passed through.

While Calder increasingly crowded the studio with mobiles and stabiles, he also equipped the house with gadgets of a more practical nature. He recycled scrap metal into household goods: aluminum lamps with necks that bent this way and that, door latches, lighting fixtures, a fire screen and andirons, ashtrays and candle holders. He outfitted the kitchen with a prodigious number of utensils: soup strainers, ladles, grills, trivets, even a chafing dish that he made out of tin cans.

A wife who could not cook probably would have been driven to despair by Calder's ceaseless production of kitchenware. Louisa, fortunately, was an excellent cook, capable of turning out hearty meals which usually included salad, cheese and wine. The kitchen was filled frequently with the fragrant aroma of roast lamb or roast beef—or roast goose, if it was a holiday. The family dined informally, usually in the kitchen or, if the weather was pleasant, outdoors under the apple tree.

Calder continued to make bigger and bigger mobiles, which became increasingly graceful in

bles a Gothic cathedral. Like a cathedral, the stabile has a tall spire, as well as a number of thin legs which curve outward like the flying buttresses on a medieval church. It is important because of the prophetic nature of its design. It could pass as a scale model for the huge, walk-through stabiles, like "Teodelapio" (page 108), that Calder created more than twenty years later. Who could have guessed that Calder eventually

shape and movement. In 1939 he was commissioned to design a mobile for the stairwell of the Museum of Modern Art in New York, an assignment that prompted him to make the delightful "Lobster Trap and Fish Tail" (page 60). This is one of his largest mobiles up to that date; spread out, it is almost ten feet in diameter.

That same year Calder made a small stabile, "Gothic Construction from Scraps," which he actually assembled from metal parings. Though it is less than three feet high, the stabile resem-

OPPOSITE: Sandy produced many of his most enchanting mobiles in his crowded Roxbury studio, shown here in 1963. He never wanted to unclutter the place for fear he might "lose something valuable—my imagination."
ABOVE: A fantastic face greets visitors to the bathroom in Roxbury.
RIGHT: An array of Calder-designed skimmers, strainers and other utensils shared kitchen space in Roxbury with a collection of pans, baskets, kettles and an antique iron stove.

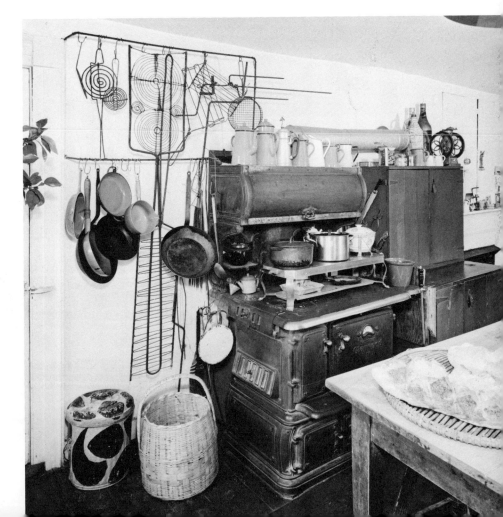

OPPOSITE: By around 1940 the wall above Louisa's dressing table was festooned with elaborate necklaces made by Sandy. Some of her bracelets and pins lie on the table top. ABOVE: Calder's boldly designed jewelry is often made of hammered brass or silver, sometimes gold. He made a wide variety of brooches, rings, necklaces, combs, earrings, buckles and tiaras.

would design sculpture that looked very much like this—but sixty and eighty feet high?

It was also an important year for Louisa. In May she gave birth (it was a Caesarean delivery this time) to a second daughter, whom they named Mary after Louisa's sister.

Turning out sculpture and tinkering with household gadgets satisfied one part of Calder's creative ambitions; another part led him at about this time to fashion a prodigious amount of jewelry out of brass, copper, silver and gold. It seems, in retrospect, that he was always interested in jewelry. As a child in Pasadena, he had made copper-wire jewelry for his sister's doll. During his years with Louisa, he had made her numerous pieces of jewelry—from her gold "engagement" ring to an impressive array of necklaces, pins and combs.

In December 1940, Calder had a one-man jewelry show at the Willard Gallery in New York. It proved conclusively that Calder had an extraordinary knack for twisting a single piece of wire into linear patterns that appeared simultaneously sophisticated and primitive. Some of the pieces were abstract: a buckle, consisting of concentric semicircles, and a bracelet with dangling spirals. There were cuff links made from a continuous piece of silver wire—starting at the center, Calder had wound the wire around in concentric circles to form one side of the link, then bent it to make a crossbar, then reversed the process to make the other side of the link. Other pieces were representational, like the mobile earrings in the shape of fish skeletons. Then there were the stylized monograms, in which the letters were contorted into such complex configurations as to be almost illegible. As one collector gloated: "His initialed things are so complicated that you can remarry and it's still all right."

Because his first show of jewelry was such a financial success, Calder tried to repeat his luck the following year with another December show, which he shrewdly timed to capture the attention of Christmas shoppers. On a Sunday, when the Willard Gallery was closed to the public, Calder

Sandy's toy car, which resembles his La Salle, is made from a cigar box and a tin can. During World War II he visited hospitalized servicemen, contributing to their occupational therapy by instructing them in how to make similar gadgets and toys from readily available materials, such as wood, wire and cloth. Some of these toys were included in an "art and therapy" exhibition at the Museum of Modern Art in 1943.

spent the whole day setting up the show. Later, Louisa informed him that while he had been arranging his ornaments, Japanese warplanes had made a surprise attack on the United States Pacific fleet, anchored at Pearl Harbor in Hawaii. The attack destroyed several ships and killed about three thousand Americans.

On Monday, December 8, 1941, the day of Calder's opening, the United States declared war on Japan, thereby entering World War II. It was hardly the most auspicious day on which to open a show of jewelry. "In spite of all," Calder noted philosophically in his autobiography, "quite a few people came to see the show."

It was not long before the Calders were drawn into the war effort. Louisa became a nurse's aide at nearby Waterbury Hospital. Calder, who had been too young to serve in World War I, discovered—much to his surprise, at age forty-three—that he was still eligible for the draft. He might have to prepare for another kind of "mobilization"—possible war duty. As it turned out, the nearest he got to the war was a military hospital where he visited wounded soldiers. Armed with hammer and shears, Calder entered the wards and tried to entertain the patients by cutting up tin cans and converting them into ashtrays and toys. His "little stunts," as he called them, were intended to "encourage" and "inspire" the wounded to make objects of a similar nature.

Because of the war, gasoline and meat were strictly rationed. The Calders, like thousands of other Americans, began to cultivate vegetables in their own "victory" garden. Nearly everything was in short supply, and Calder was particularly vexed by the aluminum shortage. Most of the country's aluminum was being turned into warplanes. In order to obtain materials for his sculpture, Calder cut up an old aluminum boat that he had made for the Roxbury pond.

Parts of that aluminum boat may have ended up as the red "leaves" in "Red Petals," a majestic standing mobile that suggests an exotic houseplant. The three-legged base, which functions like a tripod, was made from an oil boiler that he bought from a junkyard. The delicate mobile, which is suspended from the tip of the base, consists entirely of "leaves," except for one blade that is in the shape of a tulip.

Lacking his usual art materials, Calder began to experiment with new forms. The result was a series of "point-and-line" sculptures, designed to stand on a base or hang on the wall. He made them by carving and painting small bits of wood which he attached to a framework of steel wires. He called them "Constellations" (page 84), because they resembled astronomy charts, with straight lines connecting the star points. The "Constellations" are not as important historically as the mobiles, but they share some com-

83

mon themes: open forms, elegant compositions and allusions to the universe. To Calder's way of thinking, they were specifically related to the "Universes" he had made in the early 1930s.

There were many occasions during the war years when Sandy and Louisa almost felt they were back in Paris, since so many of the artists they had known in Europe were now living in the United States. As the Nazi leaders of Germany had a reputation for persecuting modern artists and consigning their art to public bonfires, many artists fled Paris before it was invaded by the German army in 1940.

Mondrian was one of the European artists who arrived in New York in 1940. He settled into a Manhattan apartment and turned it into a near-replica of his old Paris apartment—with all the colored paper rectangles on the walls. He began collecting boogie-woogie records, and seemed to thrive on New York's night life. His abstract

OPPOSITE: *Constellation with Bomb*, 1943. Wood sculpture: wood, wire and steel, 31″ x 30″ x 18″. Perls Galleries, New York.

Calder's fascination with the solar system may have originated during his childhood in Oracle, Arizona, when he and his family spent the desert evenings stargazing. His mother had a book, *The Friendly Stars*, that they used as a guide to locate heavenly bodies and constellations.

RIGHT: *Hen with Red Knife*, c. 1944. Wood sculpture: wood and steel wire, 18¹/₂″ x 8¹/₂″ x 3³/₄″. Perls Galleries.

canvases found an appreciative audience in New York, where he was able at last to sell his canvases without difficulty for about two hundred dollars each.

Duchamp was one of the last of the European artists to reach New York, arriving in 1942. For several years he had been condensing his life work into a small suitcase, which he was planning to reproduce in a limited edition. It was, in effect, a portable one-man museum, containing miniature reproductions of some of his art works (a glass flask of Paris air, a urinal and a typewriter cover) and photographic reproductions of such works as "Nude Descending a Staircase." Impersonating a cheese merchant, Duchamp made several trips through Nazi-occupied France to the port city of Marseilles, each time carrying out a batch of his miniature reproductions. When he had them all safely in Marseilles, he made his way to Portugal, where he took a boat from Lisbon to New York.

Of all the foreign artists who took refuge in the United States, Duchamp fit in most comfortably with the Americans. This was, after all, the second time around for him, as he had also waited out the First World War in New York. But most of the European refugees had a difficult time adjusting to their new life in an alien land. Despite their importance and fame in Europe, they found themselves practically unknown in the United States. Consequently, the Calders exercised their flair for Franco-American diplomacy, losing few opportunities to make the foreigners feel more at home.

In 1943 Calder received the good news that his friends and admirers on the staff of the Museum of Modern Art in New York were going to mount a retrospective exhibition of his work. Since the Modern conveyed more prestige than any other museum devoted to contemporary art, a one-man exhibition there was—and is now—regarded as a great honor. Calder was forty-five years old with a distinguished body of work behind him and, apparently, now qualified as a "mature" modern artist. His friend James Johnson Sweeney organized the show, which exposed Calder to a much larger public than any of his previous one-man exhibitions. The show opened in September and contained nearly one hundred pieces. There were early wire figures: "Josephine Baker," "The Hostess," "Helen Wills," "Acrobats." There were motorized, hanging and standing mobiles: "A Universe," "Lobster Trap and Fish Tail," "Red Petals." There were two large stabiles: "Whale," "Black Beast"; a scale model of the "Mercury Fountain"; four "Constellations" and a dozen pieces of jewelry.

As a sort of sideshow to the exhibition, Calder

presented a circus performance for an invited audience in the museum's penthouse.

The museum show was a great personal triumph for Calder. Unhappily, it was accompanied and followed by a succession of unfortunate events.

First of all, Feathers died. Returning to their Roxbury home one day, the Calders saw Feathers playing, as he often did, with the neighbors. As usual, Feathers raced after the La Salle, up the steep hill, but disappeared from sight as the car entered the driveway. Calder parked and went back to investigate. Feathers had collapsed, and nothing would revive him. Calder buried him by the pond, placing a white stone at the head of the grave.

Then the Roxbury house caught fire. At the time, Calder was in Chicago, where he was having a show, and Louisa was in New York, visiting friends. Luckily, a neighbor spotted the blaze and called out the local fire brigade, which extinguished the flames as best it could. Shortly after midnight, another neighbor noticed more flames emerging from the roof of the house, and sounded the alarm again. This time, fewer fire fighters came and they had to break in part of the roof in order to put out the fire once and for all. The fire completely destroyed the old icehouse (which Calder initially had used as a workshop),

the woodshed and a corner of the bathroom, where the toilet exploded. The following day, Louisa, who had come back from New York, and a neighbor dragged all they could salvage into the new workshop. When Calder returned from Chicago, he found not only a partly burned house, but also a studio that was cluttered with all sorts of paraphernalia, making it possible for him to misplace and "lose" things for years.

In January 1944, Mondrian was stricken with pneumonia. The seventy-one-year-old artist, whose paintings were so amazingly modern, was not so modern that he would tolerate a telephone in his apartment. When worried friends visited him, they found him in a feverish state and rushed him to a nearby hospital. Mondrian's condition deteriorated for five days, until his case was declared hopeless. During Mondrian's final hours, Calder and James Johnson Sweeney were among the small group of friends who waited silently in the hospital corridor. A couple of days later, Calder, Sweeney and Duchamp were among the scores of people in the art world who turned out to mourn the Dutch artist at his funeral service.

Mondrian is now recognized as one of the great artists of the twentieth century. Not the least of Mondrian's considerable achievements is that he opened Calder's eyes to the spirit and adventure of pure abstraction in art. If Calder had never met Mondrian, the young sculptor might never have received the impetus to make abstract art—and to set it in actual motion.

On Christmas Day of that year, the Calders were celebrating with friends in Connecticut when Nanette telephoned to say that Stirling was seriously ill in St. Luke's Hospital in Manhattan. Calder visited his father the next day and, for nearly two weeks, shuttled back and forth between Roxbury and the New York hospital. Stirling died during the first weekend of 1945, a few days before his seventy-fifth birthday.

By most standards, Stirling had had an exceptionally successful career. He won numerous awards and prizes, and was made a member of just about every academic art organization in the country. Though he was initially sympathetic toward the modern movement, his own career developed along increasingly conservative lines. At the time of his death, Stirling was so far outside the mainstream of modern art that the magazine *Art News,* in its garbled obituary, confused him with Alexander Milne Calder, describing Stirling as the man who had made the "celebrated statue of William Penn which surmounts the Philadelphia City Hall."

Alexander Stirling Calder and Piet Mondrian were as unlikely a pair of mentors as anyone could find. Yet each had a profound influence on Sandy.

Watery, c. 1947. Gouache, 22³/₄" x 30³/₄". Perls Galleries, New York.

SANDY BEGAN THINKING OF ANOTHER TRIP to Europe as soon as World War II ended in September, 1945. While he had consolidated his reputation in the United States, he had not shown his work in Paris for twelve years—long enough to be forgotten. During the fall, Duchamp examined some of Calder's recent mobiles, a few as tiny as three inches high. "Yes," Duchamp murmured, "let's mail these little objects to Carré, in Paris, and have a show." Duchamp cabled Louis Carré, a Paris dealer, and persuaded him to give Sandy an exhibition. They decided that Sandy would construct a series of mobiles and airmail them to France.

There were restrictions at the time on the size of airmail packages; they could not exceed eighteen inches in length and twenty-four inches in circumference. Sandy discovered he could mail large works, provided he could disassemble them in such a way as to fit into packages that were no more than eighteen inches long, ten inches wide and two inches thick. He could even squeeze in a nineteen-inch-long rod by inserting it on the diagonal. Before sealing each package, he stuffed in a drawing to show how the piece should be reassembled. Following this method, he constructed, dismantled and mailed enough mobiles for an entire show.

In June 1946, Sandy himself flew to Europe, making his first overseas flight. Paris appeared miraculously untouched by the war. Unlike London, which had been ravaged by German rockets and bombers, Paris looked almost exactly as it did twenty years earlier, when he first saw it. However, life in the city was drab and austere. Ordinary items like bread and wine were rationed, and people regarded themselves as lucky if they were able to obtain sausage, eggs or butter.

Sandy hung around Paris for six weeks and, through his persistence and charm, succeeded in getting the French philosopher Jean-Paul Sartre to write a preface for the brochure to the Carré show. But Carré postponed the show, so Sandy eventually flew home. Upon his return to Connecticut, he was interviewed by a local newspaper. "Paris is still the center of the art world," he declared. "In spite of the German occupation and the strict rationing and food shortage, art in all its forms is flourishing there as it did before the war."

Sandy's evaluation of the matter was almost completely wrong. After the war, the center of the art world shifted to New York, and it was there that art would flourish during the next few decades. But Sandy, losing touch with the contemporary art scene, remained an ardent fan of Paris—the city where he had his first success.

In the fall of 1946, Sandy flew again to Paris, where his show opened at Carré's in late October. Because of power cutbacks, there was no electricity every afternoon between five and six. Sandy, with characteristic ingenuity, installed a candle on the floor during that hour, placing it under a mobile with numerous small leaves. The rising heat helped the mobile rotate. Sandy gloated: "It was very fine with the shadow going around. . . ."

Sandy had never visited South America, so he and Louisa were delighted when a Brazilian architect arranged a show of Calder's work in Rio de Janeiro in 1948. Sandy shipped most of his work on ahead and, with Louisa, set off on a leisurely jaunt to South America. In Rio, the Brazilians made a great to-do over Sandy. Reporters met him at the airport, and his hosts pro-

Only Only Bird, 1952. Hanging construction: tin, wire, 14⁹/₁₀" x 41²/₁₀". The Phillips Collection, Washington, D.C.

Calder recycled ale and coffee cans to fashion this outlandish creature, whose plaid crest is cut from a Scotch-tape container. The title derives from advertising copy on one of the coffee cans: "ONLY Aborns dares reveal its complete blend because Aborns uses ONLY highest priced premium coffee and *nothing* else!"

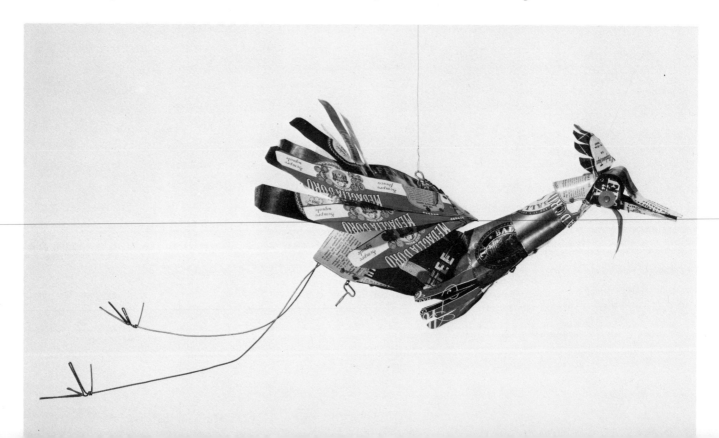

vided him with a limousine and chauffeur. Nearly a thousand people attended the gala opening of the exhibition at the Ministerio de Educaçao. Sandy assumed the opening would be a formal affair so he wore a tuxedo, which caused him considerable embarrassment when he discovered he was the only man present who was wearing one.

The show was a big hit with the public. Spec- tators wrote various remarks in the guest book, ranging from "Calder is the Mozart of space," to "How can a man who is so completely unbalanced create art which has such perfect balance?" The opening ceremonies included several lengthy statements about Calder and his art by the Brazilians. Sandy sat in the first row so he wouldn't miss a single word about himself, but since all the words were in Portuguese, which he didn't understand, he dozed off. He was more startled than embarrassed when a few news photographers woke him up so they could take his picture.

Blue-Tongued Fish, 1957. Hanging construction: metal, glass and crockery, 52" x 18". Collection Mr. and Mrs. Klaus G. Perls, New York.

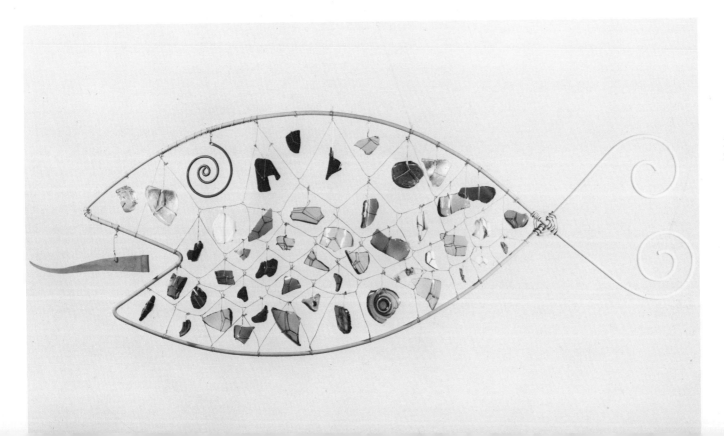

Sandy and Louisa were infatuated with Rio, the beauty of its bay, and the majestic proportions of Sugar Loaf Mountain. They admired the city's modern architecture and its broad, dazzling sidewalks with undulating patterns of colored terrazzo. They saw the sights, including a voodoo ceremony, and even learned a springy Brazilian dance called the samba. When it came time to leave, they threw a lively farewell party for which they hired a sixteen-piece samba band.

Clutching as many souvenirs and samba records as they could get their hands on, Sandy and Louisa returned to Connecticut and tried to communicate their enthusiasm for the samba to their neighbors. Sandy admitted he had difficulty in grasping the elements of the dance step, which he turned into an eccentric shuffle. As Louisa wryly observed, "Sandy dances the samba no matter *what* records we play."

In the spring of 1950, the entire Calder family sailed to France, making themselves at home in a Paris apartment. Sandra, who remembered nothing of her first visit to Paris when she was two years old, was now fifteen, and Mary, who had never been to Paris, was eleven. Sandy took with him several mobiles, which he showed in June at Galerie Maeght. This was to be the first of many shows with Aimé Maeght, who thereafter became Sandy's chief European dealer.

Soon after his show opening, Sandy took his family to Brittany in northwest France, to visit a friend who had a small summer house alongside the Tréguier River, about a mile from the sea. While staying there, the Calders explored the area in a pickup truck. On one excursion, they discovered a strange-looking house with pitched roof and dormer windows, facing the sea. The isolated house was situated on a mound near the mouth of the river. At high tide, the mound became an island. A local legend had it that a crazy woman lived there and that she kept her husband chained to an iron bedstead. The house and its romantic setting captured Sandy's imagination, and seven years later he would return to buy it.

The Calders spent part of the summer touring Finland and Sweden, then returned to Paris for a few days before heading homeward.

Back home, Sandy spent part of the fall preparing for a big exhibition of his work at the Massachusetts Institute of Technology in Cambridge. The show, which was held in December, drew praise from most of the professors. Some of the M.I.T. students, eager to show off their knowledge, theorized that all the various movements of the mobiles could be reduced to "elliptical integrals."

In the course of 1950, Sandy went to Washington, D.C., where he was being given a one-man show at the Institute of Contemporary Arts. While making the rounds of parties in the nation's capital, he met Jean Davidson, a thirty-seven-year-old journalist who covered Washington for a French news agency. The two of them hit it off immediately. One thing they had in common was that each was the son of a traditional sculptor. Davidson's father was the widely celebrated sculptor, Jo Davidson, who specialized in modeling busts of famous people.

Jean Davidson, who had been born in France and spoke French fluently, took Sandy on some hair-raising rides around Washington in his sports car. Davidson was a fanatic about speed. As a child, he used to pretend that he was the son not of Jo Davidson the sculptor, but instead, of Harley-Davidson, the motorcycle manufacturer. Later, he owned his own motorcycle and, when that proved too tame, he took up aviation.

Sandy invited Davidson to visit the Calder family at Roxbury at Christmas time. When Davidson arrived, Nanette Calder, then a vigorous eighty-five, expressed her delight at meeting the son of Jo Davidson, whose work she greatly respected. Jean Davidson responded by telling her how much he admired Sandy's work. Nanette retorted: "Oh! But you should have known Stirling—he was a sculptor!"

In the spring of 1952, Sandy again flew to Paris, this time to design the stage set for a play which a friend of his had written. The play was a flop, but Sandy's set received good notices. Louisa joined him in Paris for the opening, then the two of them went off to visit friends—the artist André Masson and his wife Rose, in Aix-en-Provence. Sandy and Louisa decided it would be a good idea for their family to spend an entire year in France; they arranged to rent a house in southern France for the following year.

During his stay in Paris, Sandy ran into the Venezuelan architect Carlos Raúl Villanueva, who was commissioning several modern artists to create special works for University City in Caracas. Villanueva had designed an auditorium for the university and he asked Sandy if he would be interested in making a large mobile for the lobby.

"I'd rather be in the main hall," Sandy said.

Villanueva told him that was out of the question because the ceiling of the main hall was going to be entirely covered with acoustical reflectors. Sandy proposed that he be allowed to design the reflectors in collaboration with the acoustical engineers. Villanueva agreed to what was, in effect, Sandy's largest commission up to that date.

Sandy consulted with an engineering firm in Cambridge, Massachusetts, as soon as he returned to the United States. Together, they came up with a bold, simple design for the acoustical reflectors. Their plan called for a series of gigantic, leaflike panels to be cut from large pieces of plywood and suspended horizontally from the ceiling like flat, cutout clouds. The panels were as long as thirty feet, and each was painted a bright, solid color. All the panels, which hung from the ceiling on cables at different heights, were tilted at various angles to deflect the sound.

"The more of your shapes," one of the engineers told Sandy, "the merrier and the louder." The result was an extremely happy collaboration between the architect, sculptor and engineers. Many visitors praised the cheerful, buoyant-looking reflectors, and one architecture writer observed that the curved panels echoed the concave curve of the cantilevered balconies, and that they seemed to perform in concert, "like trapeze artists with their nets."

Calder's growing international reputation was given still another boost when, in the summer of 1952, he was chosen to be the only sculptor representing the United States in the Venice Biennale, the international art show held every other summer in that Italian city. (The other three artists who represented the United States that year were all painters: Edward Hopper, Stuart Davis and Yasuo Kuniyoshi.) Sandy's works were se-

94

lected and installed by his old friend, James Johnson Sweeney. There were twenty-three items on view, including ten mobiles. The pieces ranged from early works in wire, such as "Josephine Baker," "Acrobats" and "Helen Wills," to a selection of mobiles and stabiles from the 1930s and 1940s. To the delight of many, Sandy won the major sculpture prize, which further established him as one of the world's most eminent artists.

During the spring of 1953, Sandy went to a New York department store to buy a couple of steamer trunks in preparation for the family's year abroad. Out of the corner of his eye, he noticed something bobbing about in the distance. To his astonishment, it turned out to be a mobile —but not one that he had made.

Although Calder's mobiles had twirled around in various parts of the world for nearly twenty years, only now were they beginning to catch on with the general public. After Sandy's success at the Venice Biennale, novelty companies quickly capitalized on his invention. As *Time* magazine noted later in the year: "Until recently, hardly anyone thought of these dangling doodles as suitable for the living room. But this year, with artists designing mobiles for commercial production, they seem to be growing into a national fad. A whole new minor industry is turning out thousands every day, from $1 up." (Sandy's mobiles were priced according to size, from $150 to $3,000.)

A Chicago company manufactured a mobile, called "Sky," in which a pair of crescent moons bobbed around a sun. A Manhattan firm specialized in seasonal mobiles, such as "Santa," which featured Santa Claus, reindeer and an angel, all suspended from a crescent moon, and "Spring," a pastel concoction of rabbits, birds, butterflies and flowers. Other companies produced a "circus" collection of mobiles, with acrobats and animals, and "nursery" mobiles with an assortment of storybook characters.

In addition, magazine articles and books appeared, instructing their readers in how to make mobiles. By 1959, *Sunset*, the "Magazine of Western Living," published a do-it-yourself article, headlined: "Why Not Driftwood Mobiles?" None of these imitators flattered Sandy. As he pungently put it: "They nauseate me." He might have looked more favorably upon the mobile manufacturers if they had properly credited him with the invention. What angered him most of all was that he could not collect a single cent in royalties. He held no patent on his invention— and he now imagined that it was making fortunes for others.

In June, the Calder family sailed to France.

Sandy picked up a new automobile, a Citroën, in Paris, then drove the family to Aix-en-Provence, where they settled into a rented country house. The place was so rustic that they had to pump their water by hand and do without electricity. Sandy converted the old carriage shed into a studio and installed a worktable. The makeshift studio was small and poorly equipped for making sculpture, so Calder used it to paint fanciful pictures in gouache—a water-based pigment that suited his easygoing personality better than oils.

Calder's gouaches combine the cheerful, primitive vigor of children's drawings with the sophisticated simplification of poster designs. Employing bold shapes and bright, solid colors, Sandy covered the large sheets of paper with his usual array of representational and abstract motifs—faces, animals, starfish, pyramids, spirals, disks and squiggles. His technique consisted of laying the paper on the table and inundating it with water. As the paper absorbed the water and began to dry, he took a brush, loaded it with black ink or colored pigment and quickly drew whatever forms came to mind, improvising as he went along and taking advantage of accidents that occured along the way.

When he was not in his carriage-shed studio, Sandy was touring the surrounding countryside with Louisa, looking up old friends. One day

95

they decided to seek out Jean Davidson, who had left Washington, D.C., to resettle in France. They thought the best way to track him down was to first locate his brother, who was living in Saché, a town in the central part of France.

In Saché, Sandy and Louisa inquired at the post office for directions to the house of Jean Davidson's brother, a mansion that had once belonged to Jo Davidson. The house, they were told, was on the other side of the Indre River and they would have to cross a narrow bridge to get there. Sandy and Louisa resumed their drive, only to see a familiar-looking sports car flash by in front of them. It was Jean.

After a joyous greeting, Davidson led the Calders to a nearby old mill on an island in the middle of the Indre River, about half a mile from his brother's house. The mill was three stories high, with each floor consisting of one large room. Davidson had recently acquired the property and planned to convert the mill into a house.

Sandy and Louisa returned to Saché in November for Jean Davidson's grand housewarming. They were greatly impressed by the mill's dramatic transformation. Davidson had built an elevated fireplace about three feet above the floor

OPPOSITE: *Three Moons, Spirals, and Curves,* c. 1949. Gouache, 23″ x 31″. Perls Galleries, New York.
LEFT: Sandy, painting gouaches in Saché, 1966.

and over a window, so that one could simultaneously watch a roaring fire and the churning water of the river below. Seeing how envious Sandy was, Davidson told him, "You, too, must buy a mill."

Later, Davidson drove Sandy around the countryside to look at various water mills and windmills, but Sandy saw nothing that caught his fancy. Then he learned, to his surprise, that Davidson owned three other properties in addition to the mill. These were a small house on an island in the river, and two other houses across the road. One of the houses had a spectacular cellarlike room with a dirt floor and an old wine press installed in a cavity of the rock wall. It was too dark to see much of anything, because most of the doors and windows were filled in with loose stones.

"I much prefer this to any mill we've seen," Sandy told Davidson, thinking to himself: "I will make mobiles of cobwebs and propel them with bats."

Davidson proposed a swap. He still owed Sandy money for some artworks he had bought, and he had no use for this particular house, so he suggested, "I'll sell it to you for what I owe and you'll make me a few more mobiles." Sandy readily agreed to this cashless transaction. They returned to Davidson's mill, carried in a workbench, and Sandy started working off his part of

the deal right on the spot, snipping and hammering bits of metal in front of a large window overlooking the river.

In addition to producing sufficient mobiles for Davidson, Sandy worked diligently on his new house, which needed repairs from top to bottom. But the task was more than he could handle; so he hired a crew of masons, plumbers and carpenters, put Davidson in charge of them, and drove off with his family to spend a week or so in Brittany.

Sandy received a letter about this time, inviting him to make a mobile for the Middle East Airlines office in Beirut, Lebanon. He and Louisa welcomed the opportunity to visit the Middle East, so the following January, the entire family sailed from Marseilles on a Greek steamer. In Beirut, Sandy was provided with a workroom in the Middle East Airlines office, and he set about making the required mobile. During the month the Calders were based in Beirut, they made several sightseeing trips to the sites of ancient cities in Lebanon, Syria and Jordan.

By the time the Calders flew back to France, they were impatient to move into the Saché house. Though the house was not yet finished, they shipped all their goods from Aix, then set off in the Citroën to their new home. They were delighted to see that all the stones had been removed from the windows and doorways, and there were new doors and sashes. The plumber was still working with the drainpipes and the septic tank, and the mason had not yet finished plastering the new ceiling in the lower room. The dirt floor had been leveled, then carefully laid with tiles. Once it was finally renovated and furnished, the Saché house was strikingly handsome. One French magazine praised Sandy for preserving the rustic character of the building, while outfitting it with such American "luxuries" as central heating and modern bathroom

Sandy and Louisa, leaving their Saché house on their way to market, 1964.

fixtures. The magazine also endorsed the way in which everything functional was left exposed and treated as decoration.

Eventually, it was time to return to the United States. The year abroad had been eventful; the Calders had acquired a new home and made their first trip to the Middle East. Sandy even managed to put on a show of his gouaches in Paris during spring, 1954. As summer approached, Louisa and Mary returned to the United States

Sidewalk, 1970. Black and white terrazzo, 15' x 75', Madison Avenue between 78th and 79th Streets, New York.

Calder's overlapping initials are integrated into the energetic design, inspired in part by his memories of the sidewalks in Rio de Janeiro.

by boat, and Sandy returned a month later. Sandra, who had just turned nineteen, decided to stay behind and continue her education in France.

That year, the New York art dealer Klaus Perls wrote to Sandy, offering to be his representative. Perls and his wife Dolly had recently moved into a five-story Madison Avenue townhouse, which served as their gallery and home. Though Perls specialized in expensive, long-established School of Paris artists, he saw great potential in Calder. Sandy visited the Perlses, looked the building over, and declared: "I'll fill the place for you." It was the beginning of a long, amiable and profitable relationship. Starting in 1956, Sandy exhibited annually at the Perls Galleries. Several years later, Sandy devised a sculpture garden with its own Calder murals behind the Perls building; it served as a showcase for Calder stabiles. In 1970, Sandy designed a terrazzo sidewalk (page 100) for the front of the Perls building. Klaus and Dolly Perls were delighted to encounter Calder designs all around their living and working quarters.

In return, Klaus Perls assumed virtually all of Sandy's financial and exhibition management. Perls assembled archives and slides to document Sandy's art, and also suggested that Sandy devise a "signature" with which to sign the metal sculpture. The result was the monogram ⚆, which Sandy subsequently embossed on his constructions. Perls also hinted that it was time to raise Sandy's prices. "What?" Sandy exclaimed. "You think you can get a thousand dollars for a mobile?"

Since Sandy liked to travel, he could scarcely turn down an invitation to visit India. Shortly before leaving France, he received a letter from an Indian architect who wanted to acquire some of his works but, because of government regulations, could not export money. She inquired whether he would like to swap some art for a trip to India. Sandy was no doubt delighted that his artworks had at last become a sort of currency—which could be bartered for a house or a trip halfway around the world—and quickly accepted the offer. In January 1955, Sandy and Louisa left New York for India, flying by way of Europe. They landed in Bombay and took a twelve-hour train trip north to Ahmedabad, where they were met by their hostess and a retinue of servants. Then they were driven to the family's beautifully landscaped, nineteen-acre compound and installed in a separate house of their own, one of several houses on the estate. A workbench was put in the garden and Sandy, who had picked up some metal and wire in Bombay, went to work on his share of the bargain.

After their stay in Ahmedabad, Sandy and Louisa toured India, visiting Delhi, Calcutta and Jaipur. Louisa scoured the markets for bargains and returned to the United States, two months after starting out, laden down with textiles, saris, embroideries and even some Bengalese jodhpurs.

In August, Sandy flew to Caracas, where Carlos Raúl Villanueva had arranged a show for him at the Museo de Bellas Artes. Amazingly, the exhibition was a total sellout. Louisa was supposed to join Sandy in Venezuela, but she was prevented by a violent hurricane which swept through New England, killing hundreds of people and causing extensive property damage. When Sandy finally got through to Louisa by telephone, he was greatly relieved to learn she was safe and that their house had not been washed away in a flood.

After his return from Venezuela, Sandy gathered in the kitchen with Louisa and both daughters, who had just come back from France. "Sandra wants to marry Jean," Louisa informed him. Sandy didn't know what to say. Sandra was only twenty, while Jean Davidson, at forty-one, was a widely traveled, sophisticated man. Despite his misgivings, Sandy kissed Sandra and gave his consent.

Sandra was eager to rush back to France, so her parents put her on a plane as soon as possible and promised to follow within a few weeks. The wedding took place in Saché in late October. Sandra went to live in the mill over the river. One year later, she gave birth to a son, Shawn Davidson.

During 1957, Sandy and Louisa summered once again in Brittany and talked about that curious house at the mouth of the river. According to the current rumor, the chained husband had died and his vengeful widow wished to sell the place. Sandy set out to investigate with Jean Davidson. As they approached the house, they encountered a young, deaf-mute man, cultivating potatoes. Sandy inquired about the damaged portions of the building and received a capsule history—all in pantomime—of the Allied invasion of France in 1944. Evidently, portions of the house had been demolished by bombs during the war and had had to be rebuilt. Sandy and Davidson were invited inside, where they found an elderly woman lying in bed with a heavy bag of sand on her stomach, a supposed remedy for stomach pains. Eventually, the woman expressed her willingness to sell the place and Sandy agreed to buy it—his second house in France. At last he possessed the house that had first attracted his attention seven years earlier. Sandy and Louisa installed electricity and new plumbing, and began spending part of each summer there.

Sandy and Louisa might have moved permanently to France at that time; but they felt obliged to remain, at least part of the year, near two members of the family. Their daughter Mary was still in school in New England and Nanette Calder did not like to be left all alone in Roxbury. Although she was essentially in good health, Nanette developed alarming symptoms whenever Sandy went away for any length of time. Sandy made light of her sudden illnesses. "As soon as I reach the deathbed," he joked to one visitor, "she's had a miraculous recovery."

Until 1957, Sandy received few commissions for large works. Suddenly, he found himself involved simultaneously in three big projects for different countries—France, Belgium and the United States. He had three different metal shops in Connecticut working for him at once, and he began to feel like an industrialist.

In one shop, he oversaw the construction of a thirty-foot-high standing mobile, "The Spiral," commissioned for an area outside UNESCO headquarters in Paris. In the second shop, he and his crew built a twenty-one-foot-high motorized mobile, "The Whirling Ear," commissioned for the United States Pavilion at the Brussels World's Fair. This mobile, which still stands in Brussels as a gift from the United States, has only two elements. The top element is a sheet of aluminum cut into an irregular shape and bent into a continuous curved plane like a giant potato chip. It rests on a solid base that conceals a motor. Initially, Sandy wanted the aluminum sheet to make two revolutions a minute, but before the piece was finished, he changed his mind and reduced the speed to one revolution a minute. In the third shop, Sandy supervised the construction of ".125," the huge mobile for Kennedy International Airport in New York.

With these three important commissioned works, all put in place during 1958, Sandy received widespread attention, bringing him greater popularity than ever. Governments, corporations and institutions which normally shied away from modern art could sponsor Calder's playful, easy-to-understand abstractions and succeed in pleasing almost everybody. From here on, Calder's sculpture would become increasingly visible in public places.

Sandy received additional attention when he won first prize for sculpture at the 1958 Carnegie Institute International, a huge show of contemporary art in Pittsburgh. Sandy was awarded the prize for a large mobile, about twenty-eight by twenty-eight feet, that he designed to hang over the Institute's stairwell. After the show, the mobile was bought by a collector and donated to the Pittsburgh Airport.

When Sandy arrived at the airport to help install the mobile, he was greeted by several journalists. One reporter asked, "How long did it take you to make that?"

"Two or three months," Sandy replied. Then he considered the lifetime of experience that led to the making of that mobile. "Hey," he said, "it took me thirty years!"

10 AT THE AGE OF SIXTY, SANDY BEGAN turning out a multitude of large stabiles that proved he was as inventive as ever. From their first appearance in 1958, the large stabiles were an instant success. It was not long before Calder's gigantic constructions began popping up in public places all over North America and Europe.

A Calder stabile consists of several plates of heavy metal, cut into various shapes, then angled against one another and bolted together. In most cases, the stabiles are painted black. Frequently, they rest on graceful, leglike supports, which arch high enough in the air for spectators to walk under. Although the stabiles are station-ary, they sometimes seem capable of motion because their graceful contours change considerably as the spectator walks around them.

Like the mobiles, the stabiles are abstract, but may suggest plant or animal forms. Many suggest fantastic beasts with multiple legs, craning necks and curling tails. But however much the stabiles may resemble colossal creatures, they are not for one moment threatening or ferocious-looking. Like so much of Calder's work, the stabiles seem to possess a spirit that is gentle, congenial and whimsical.

Although Calder's stabiles came into full flower during the 1960s, the idea had been germinating at least as far back as 1937. In that year, Sandy made "Whale" (*left*), a sixty-eight-inch-high, black stabile, balanced with seeming precariousness upon two points and a length of

LEFT: *Whale II,* 1964 (replica after the original of 1937). Stabile: painted sheet steel, supported by a log of wood, 68" x 69$\frac{1}{2}$" x 45$\frac{3}{8}$". The Museum of Modern Art, New York; gift of the artist.

This early stabile is by no means a literal portrayal of a whale. But its dynamic, undulating contours convey the streamlined form and supple strength of this largest of marine mammals, thrashing its powerful tail above water. OPPOSITE: Sandy in the enormous studio he designed for himself in Saché, 1966.

weathered log. Although the log actually helps support the stabile, it contributes to the impression that the metal construction, although motionless, is capable of bobbing and rolling. The undulating contours and surfaces of the metal plates add to the overall impression of a twisting and turning marine mammal, vigorously thrashing its tail as it prepares to dive out of sight.

For more than twenty years, "Whale" seemed to be a curious, offbeat example of Calder's work. But that perspective began to change in 1958 when an architect friend, Eliot Noyes, offered to buy "Black Beast"—another early stabile that Sandy had made in 1940. The original "Black Beast" was made in a light-gauge metal which seemed good enough at the time. But now that Sandy finally had a buyer for the piece, he decided to remake it in quarter-inch iron plate, which is heavier and more durable. He took "Black Beast" to a metal shop near his home in Connecticut, where skilled workmen translated the original model into a sturdier version.

The success of this project encouraged Sandy to make other large stabiles in heavy-plate metal. After first making a scale model, he cut a full-scale paper pattern which he took to one of the Connecticut metal shops. There, the workers—under Calder's supervision—used the paper pattern as a guide to cut out the metal plates. "It's just like what tailors do," Sandy said.

In the winter of 1958, Calder had his first show of large stabiles in New York at Perls Galleries. Despite their large size, three of the stabiles sold. Afterward, Sandy sent about ten large stabiles to Paris for a February show at Galerie Maeght. Aimé Maeght was so enthusiastic about this development in Calder's work that he bought every single piece in the show for possible later resale, the first time any dealer had ever done that with Sandy's work. During the following year, large stabiles were sold to museums in Caracas, Houston and Chicago.

In May 1959, Calder shipped some large stabiles from Roxbury to Rio de Janeiro, where he was to have a one-man exhibition at the new modern art museum in September. When September came, Sandy and Louisa flew from Paris to Rio, and then returned to Roxbury with a load of new samba records. They immediately announced their plan to return to Rio in February to see the famous annual carnival.

Nanette Calder was upset by this news. "If you go again," she said, "I may die." Sandy and Louisa went anyway. Nanette managed to survive until their return. But the following month she was striken by a sudden illness and died in a Connecticut hospital at the age of ninety-three.

The next major shift in the Calder household occurred in April 1961, when twenty-one-year-old Mary married a young man named Howard

Rower. With both parents gone and both daughters married, Sandy might have been expected to take things easy. Instead, he settled down to work harder than ever. It was as if he had caught a second wind, impelling him to enter one of his most productive creative periods.

In Saché, Sandy was now inspired to build a large studio on a hilltop about a half-mile away from his house. There was only one drawback—the hilltop was not his. As it turned out, the section of land he wanted belonged to fourteen different people, each of whom owned a small, often irregular, piece. The property was like a crazy quilt. Thanks to his persistence, Sandy eventually acquired all the various pieces of land.

From Roxbury, Sandy sent drawings, showing what kind of studio he wanted, to Jean Davidson, who supervised the project. Calder's design was simple, almost austere. The studio walls were composed of rugged fieldstone, the floor was wooden, and the pitched roof was covered with slate tiles. In one respect, the new studio was like an enlarged version of the Roxbury studio—two walls consisted almost entirely of windows. But the Saché studio was much larger: thirty-three by ninety-eight feet. Outside the studio bulldozers were engaged to produce a flat terrace where Calder could display large pieces of sculpture.

Once the studio was built, Calder was not inclined to make much use of it. Perhaps the barnlike interior was too vast and uncluttered. Possibly his imagination was more easily triggered by makeshift, cramped quarters. (He once told a visitor to his Roxbury studio that he never tidied it up because "I might lose something valuable—my inspiration.") Sandy complained that the Saché studio was a "nuisance" to get to, so he did virtually nothing there. Consequently, the Saché studio became a repository and display room for work that was made elsewhere.

In 1962, Sandy was honored with a retrospective show at the Tate Gallery in London, and was commissioned to make a work for an outdoor sculpture show in Spoleto, Italy. From Roxbury, he sent over a scale model and detailed sketches for a large stabile that ultimately stood some fifty-nine feet tall and weighed thirty tons. Although the piece is named "Teodelapio" after a onetime duke of Spoleto, it seems more suggestive of a stylized animal with a triangular face. To some viewers, it resembles a colossal black cat with a pinched waist, fat haunches and a straight-up tail. Because the stabile spans a crossroads near the railroad station at one entrance to the medieval mountaintop town (page 108), its "torso" had to be high enough for automobiles to drive under the arches.

"Teodelapio" was constructed by an Italian steel company, and erected with the aid of two shipyard cranes. As the piece was being constructed, however, it became apparent that reinforcements were needed. The scale model had been structurally sound, but the huge blowup in scale created new, unanticipated problems. The enlarged version was subject to a more formidable set of stresses. It had to withstand high winds and resist the vibrations produced by train and automobile traffic.

Luckily, Sandy's old friend, James Johnson Sweeney, was in Spoleto to check on the pro-

Teodelapio, 1962. Stabile: painted steel plate, 59' h. Spoleto, Italy.
  The first of Calder's giant stabiles, this thirty-ton work spans a crossroads near the railroad station.

gress of "Teodelapio." He sent Calder a postcard saying, "Come quick, danger." Sandy rushed from Saché to Spoleto to discuss the best way to reinforce the stabile. It was decided to stiffen the large metal plates by adding flanges—in this case thin "ribs" of steel, attached perpendicularly.

"Teodelapio" encouraged Calder to think big. He knew now that he could make stabiles much larger than previously, providing he drew on the

Calder at the Biémont ironworks in Tours, France, discussing the placement of the ribs in *Triangles and Arches* (1965), now at Empire State Plaza, Albany, New York.

experience and know-how of professional engineers and ironworkers. He decided to find a steel-plate company in the Saché area to make his structures. With Jean Davidson, he drove to Tours, about fifteen miles from Saché, and visited an ironworks known as Etablissements Biémont. The Biémont factory seemed to have all the necessary equipment. It was outfitted with machines for grinding and crimping metal, as well as machines with rollers for putting curves into heavy metal sheets. There was a labor force of about eighty people, including technicians, draftsmen and metalworkers. The draftsmen were able to enlarge a scale model mathematically with extraordinary precision. By comparison, Calder's previous method of making full-scale paper patterns seemed almost primitive.

The Biémont people did not appear particularly anxious to have Sandy's business, but he returned anyway—with eight models for stabiles. "All I had to do," he recalled, "was have enough nerve to tell them how big I wanted them."

Le Guichet, 1963. Stabile: painted steel plate, 22' w. Lincoln Center for the Performing Arts, New York; gift of Howard and Jean Lipman.

The contours of this stabile change dramatically as the spectator moves around it. The irregular hole in one plate prompted the title, French for "box office."

111

When Sandy returned to Saché in January 1963, the eight stabiles were near completion. But the stabiles needed bracing. The larger scale increased the risk that the seams and joints might buckle. The obvious solution was ribs and gussets. Ribs are thin blades of metal affixed to a metal sheet to make it more rigid; a gusset is a triangular metal insert, butting into two surfaces, strengthening the area where the two metal sheets are joined. "When a plate seems flimsy," Sandy remarked, "I put a rib on it, and if the relation between two plates is not rigid, I put a gusset between them . . . . you invent the bracing as you go, depending on the form of each object." In every case, the ribs and gussets had to be positioned so that they harmonized visually with the overall composition.

Two of the Biémont-made stabiles—"Guillotine for Eight" and "Bucephalus"—were sent to New York for inclusion in a huge retrospective exhibition of Calder's work at the Solomon R. Guggenheim Museum. The show, which opened in November 1964, contained approximately 350 works and filled the entire museum. "Guillotine for Eight," valued at about $100,000, was the largest stabile in the show, nearly twenty-two

Spring, 1928. Wire sculpture, 94¹/₂" h. The Solomon R. Guggenheim Museum, New York.

feet high; it was installed in the rotunda of the museum. "Bucephalus," named after the favorite horse of Alexander the Great, is one of Calder's most elegant stabiles. Like Alexander's horse, which was known for its legendary speed, Calder's "Bucephalus" gives the impression of fleet, streamlined movement.

While tracking down older works to include in the Guggenheim show, Sandy came across his early wire figures, "Spring" and "Romulus and Remus" (*left* and *below*). They had been flattened out and put away since 1929. Sandy unraveled the wire pieces, hammered out the kinks,

bent them into shape once again and discovered, much to his pleasure, that he liked them more than ever. "I'd always thought these particularly humorous," he said, "but now they looked like

Romulus and Remus, 1928. Wire sculpture, 31" x 112" x 30". The Solomon R. Guggenheim Museum, New York.

Thirty-five years after he had crushed them flat and packed them away, Sandy unraveled two of his early wire sculptures, *Spring* and *Romulus and Remus,* for inclusion in his retrospective exhibition at the Guggenheim Museum in 1964. Both the young woman and the she-wolf have nipples made of wooden door stops. According to ancient legend, the twin boys, Romulus and Remus, were adopted by the she-wolf, then set out to found the city of Rome.

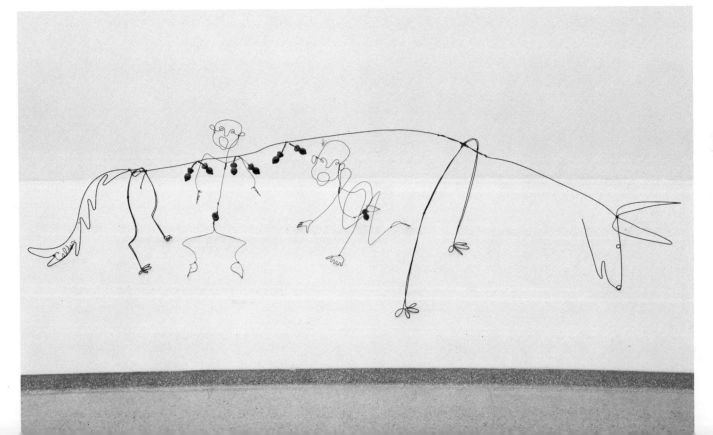

good sculpture—after thirty-five years in the closet." The following year he donated them to the Guggenheim, and the two works are now part of the museum's permanent collection.

To crown the Guggenheim show, Sandy specially designed a new, thirty-five-foot-long mobile to dangle below the museum's dome. This was "Ghost"—the stately white mobile that now hangs over the grand staircase of the Philadelphia Museum.

Sandra and Jean Davidson, accompanied by their two children, arrived in New York in mid-December to see the Guggenheim show and to spend Christmas in Roxbury. Sandy managed to tour the exhibition with Louisa, both their daughters and all four grandchildren—Shawn and Andrea Davidson and Holton and Alexander Rower. It was a joyful occasion for the entire family. At the time, Sandy said, "I suppose a lot of the toys I've made have been done with these kids in mind, but they're for myself, really."

The Guggenheim exhibition was a huge success, the most popular show in the museum's history. The show was extended until the end of

Sandy and Louisa with their daughters, sons-in-law and grandchildren in Roxbury, 1964. *Left to right:* Howard Rower, Alexander Rower, Sandy, Louisa, Holton Rower, Mary Calder Rower, Andrea Davidson, Sandra Calder Davidson, Jean Davidson and Shawn Davidson.

January 1965, and the total attendance during the eighty-day period was more than 215,000. After the show closed at the Guggenheim, it traveled to Milwaukee, St. Louis, Des Moines, Ottawa and Paris.

Sandy returned to Saché in January 1965, and within a few days began to write his autobiography with the help of Jean Davidson. Almost daily from mid-January through May, Sandy dictated his memoirs for an hour or so, and the result was published the following year. Calder's autobiography is a delightful record of his life, packed with entertaining stories about himself and the people he knew. Not surprisingly, he was reticent on the subject of his own art, which he let speak for itself. In any case, the book splendidly conveys Calder's congeniality, good humor and zest for life.

During the same period that Sandy was dictating his memoirs, he was contemplating a commission to design a stabile for a new building at the Massachusetts Institute of Technology in Cambridge. Eventually he devised a scale model for the structure he would call "The Big Sail." Sandy took his model to Biémont to be enlarged. Since the finished stabile was to be forty feet high, it was decided that Biémont should make an intermediate scale model to check stability. The intermediate model was built to one-fifth final scale—in this case, eight feet tall. "You can wobble it," Sandy said, "and see where it gives, where the vibrations occur, and then put your reinforcements there." The intermediate model helped avoid any last-minute discoveries of structural weaknesses.

In this fashion, the design kinks were worked out even before the final version was started. Even so, Sandy wanted to see that final version assembled at the factory to make sure everything looked right. "I had to see it erected to know whether it worked," he explained. "The erection was achieved in two days with the aid of a fifty-foot crane. Every part fell into place perfectly, bolt for bolt, as on the working model." The large stabile was then disassembled and shipped to Boston, where once again it was erected without incident.

At the time it was put up, "The Big Sail" was Calder's largest stabile in North America. But it was soon dwarfed by larger works—a sixty-seven-foot-high stabile that dominated the site of Expo '67 in Montreal, and a seventy-two-foot-high stabile commissioned in connection with the 1968 Olympics in Mexico City.

By the late 1960s, Calder's large stabiles had been installed successfully in so many cities throughout the world that he was the obvious choice for the United States government's pilot program to subsidize sculpture in various urban centers. The subsidies came from the recently created National Endowment for the Arts. Sandy received a $125,000 commission to create a large stabile (*opposite*) for a downtown plaza in Grand Rapids, Michigan—the first American city to receive a NEA sculpture grant.

At first, the project generated controversy. Some citizens preferred to have a fountain, while others were simply opposed to modern sculpture of any kind. To drum up public support for the stabile, the local museum and state college put on shows of Calder's art. Department-store windows displayed huge photographs of the sculptor at work. A local bank sponsored a thirty-minute color film on the artist, which was shown on television; and a scale model of the proposed stabile was displayed on the actual site.

The stabile, titled "La Grande Vitesse" (also known as "The Grand Rapids"), is painted a bright orange-red that some call "Calder Red."

La Grande Vitesse, 1969. Stabile: painted steel plate, 55' w. Calder Plaza, Grand Rapids, Michigan.

The people of Grand Rapids are proud of their forty-two-ton stabile, painted in brilliant "Calder Red," which functions as the festive centerpiece in a revitalized downtown area. In 1974 Calder designed an abstract mural for the roof of a nearby three-story building; the mural is visible from higher floors in neighboring buildings.

It was fabricated by the Biémont factory and, like "The Big Sail," was fully erected in France, then disassembled, shipped and reassembled at its permanent location.

Dedicated in June 1969, "La Grande Vitesse" quickly became a focal point of community pride and a major impetus toward renovating the downtown area. Its success helped inspire Gerald R. Ford, then the minority leader of the House of Representatives, to support, rather than oppose, appropriations for the National Endowment for the Arts. Earlier, Ford had taken a dim view of federal funding of the arts. But Grand Rapids was Ford's hometown, and when he realized how the Calder stabile "helped to regenerate a city," Ford became a vocal supporter of the federal arts program.

Today, the place occupied by "La Grande Vitesse" is known as Calder Plaza. The stabile is pictured on the sides of the city's garbage-disposal trucks, and all of their fire engines have been repainted "Calder Red."

Because Calder produced monumental stabiles in such profusion during the 1960s, one might think he did nothing else. In fact, he kept up a virtually ceaseless production of mobiles, gouaches and prints. He even managed to find a new outlet for his amazing energy when he masterminded a theatrical enterprise in 1968.

In Italy, the artistic director of the Rome Opera House invited Calder to design the decor for a ballet. Sandy—with his customary knack for turning simple requests into bigger, more challenging projects—replied that he would prefer to create an abstract theatrical spectacle without dancers. He said the idea for such a project had been "smoldering" in him for almost thirty-six years. To his surprise, his suggestion was received enthusiastically. Before this, no one had ever put an entire theater and crew at Sandy's disposal and, except for his own circus performances, he had never been in total control of a theatrical work.

Sandy arrived in Rome with a few tiny models for mobiles and a number of sketches. The theater provided him with a small workshop, and, for fifteen days, Sandy worked every morning, designing mobiles, drop curtains and gouaches. It was exhilarating, but also exhausting. Sandy lamented that he had not been asked to produce this "entertainment" ten years earlier. "I am tired now," he said.

Despite his claim to fatigue, Sandy's designs showed his characteristic vitality and youthfulness. The festive production, titled "Work in Progress," was performed for ten consecutive evenings in March. It consisted of several episodes that narrated, in an abstract sort of way, the creation of the universe—all of which took place to the sound of electronic music by modern Italian composers. As *Newsweek* described it:

The nineteen-minute work is a cosmic romp that begins with a galaxy of mobiles high above the stage like the universe before genesis. On the white screen of Part Two, the blue of the sea is projected, across which swim black sea creatures and giant red starfish. The firmament has been divided. Then comes land, with birds of every hue, followed by man—fourteen bicyclists in brightly colored stretch suits.

Finale: In the next to last part, dominated by a black pyramid and an enormous jolly sun beneath which a man waved a long red flag, Calder seemed to be noting the first stirrings of religion and politics. . . . In this finale, a heaven and earth of mobiles and stabiles, of objects seeking and finding innocent and joyful communion, Calder once more affirmed his faith in the human spirit and his belief that art is the highest expression of man's imagination.

The opening-night audience cheered the performance and some spectators called it the most stimulating theater production in Italy in more than fifty years. After Sandy saw his work performed on stage, he remarked: "I ought to have called it 'My Life in Nineteen Minutes.'"

11 As his seventy-fifth birthday approached in 1973, Sandy became increasingly irritable whenever he felt people were wasting his time. His work was all that mattered now. Though he might appear to outsiders to lead an idle, carefree life, he usually worked seven days a week. He rose daily at 6 A.M. in order to get an early start on his chores, and his only concession to old age was that he went to bed early. When he was not making art, he was engaged in related activities

Whether they were in Roxbury, as shown here in 1964, or Saché, Sandy and Louisa had a seemingly endless succession of visitors to fit into their busy schedules.

Sandy and Louisa actively protested American involvement in the war in Vietnam. They are shown here as they appeared at an antiwar march in New York in April 1967.

—taking care of his business correspondence, visiting fabrication plants, conferring with architects and money people, and inspecting sites for future mobiles and stabiles. Sandy's art was big business.

Sandy's health presented serious problems. Though he still appeared robust, he had suffered a series of strokes which made it difficult for him to walk and talk. His doctors prescribed pills to keep his hands from shaking, and they also tried to restrict his wine drinking to only a half-bottle with each meal. But Sandy liked wine far too much to follow the doctors' orders. Family meals often became battles between Sandy and Louisa, who complained that the combination of wine and pills made him woozy and forgetful. Louisa also fretted about the possibility that Sandy would become incapacitated and confined to a

121

wheelchair. How, she wondered, would she ever get him up and down stairs?

Though he was universally acknowledged as the inventor of the mobile, Sandy was easily irritated by anyone who imitated his mobiles. He felt that his mobiles had been copied, at great profit, not only by novelty manufacturers and authors of how-to-make-mobiles books, but also by the younger generation of sculptors in the 1950s and 1960s who made kinetic (moving, often electrified) constructions. Sandy had never been particularly tolerant toward other artists—certainly not toward any sculptor who might be considered a rival—but he was unusually harsh toward younger artists. Perhaps he had been poor too long and thought they had it too easy. On occasion Sandy even hired lawyers to threaten artists who he felt were imitating him.

Louisa contributed to some peace groups and charitable organizations, and both she and Sandy strongly opposed American involvement in the Vietnam war. They participated in peace demonstrations and, in 1965, Sandy went with a group of artists to Washington to protest the

OPPOSITE AND RIGHT: *Stegosaurus,* 1973. Stabile: painted steel plate, 50' h. Alfred E. Burr Memorial Mall, Hartford, Connecticut; gift of the Trustees of the Ella Burr Mc-Manus Fund.

The stegosaurus was a ten-ton vegetarian dinosaur that used to prowl Colorado and Wyoming.

war. On January 2, 1966, they sponsored a full-page ad in *The New York Times* to condemn the escalating war, calling for "an end to hypocrisy, self-righteousness, self-interest, expediency, distortion and fear, wherever they exist." In a two-page ad, published in *The New York Times* on May 31, 1972, Sandy and Louisa joined with others to call for an end to American participation in the Indochina war, and the impeachment of President Nixon on the grounds that his conduct of the war was unconstitutional.

Sandy's outspoken criticism of the United States government generated controversy, and some accused him of lacking patriotism. "I don't have much patriotism," he allowed. "Trying to get your country to do what you think is right, that's what I would consider patriotism."

Calder frequently designed and donated posters for various causes. He created posters opposing the Vietnam war, supporting George McGovern's 1972 candidacy for United States

123

president, and promoting environmental preservation. In the mid-1970s, he contributed a series of posters to benefit Amnesty International, a human-rights organization that works for the abolition of torture and the release of political prisoners in more than one hundred countries.

During his seventy-fifth year, Sandy found himself involved in an extraordinary number of monumental projects, having received major commissions to make large mobiles or stabiles for Philadelphia, Los Angeles, Fort Worth, Hartford, Chicago, Detroit and Washington, D.C. For a Hartford mall beside the city hall, Calder designed a fifty-foot-high stabile (pages 122, 123). The red-orange work is named "Stegosaurus," after the armored dinosaurs that once roamed what is now Colorado and Wyoming.

In 1974, Sandy designed a $250,000 stabile, titled "Four Arches," which rises forty-five feet above a plaza alongside the Security Pacific National Bank skyscraper in downtown Los Angeles. The United States government paid $325,000 for a bright red, three-legged, fifty-three-foot-high stabile, "Flamingo," erected in Chicago's Federal Center Plaza. In addition to the large stabiles for Hartford, Chicago and Los Angeles, Sandy designed two colossal mobiles: One is a seventy-foot, black-red-and-blue mobile that commands a three-story-high space in the sky-

One of the special events of the 31st Paris Air Show at Le Bourget Airport in May 1975 was Sandy—in person—painting an engine cover on the starboard side of Braniff's *Flying Colors*.

lighted central court of the East Building of the National Gallery of Art in Washington, D.C. (page 64); the other, motorized piece, "White Cascade," is the largest of all Calder mobiles—about one hundred feet high—and it revolves within a skylight-covered court inside the Federal Reserve Bank in Philadelphia.

Perhaps Calder's most unusual commission was to paint an airplane for the Texas-based airline, Braniff International. The airline wanted to promote its flights to South America and concluded it could get maximum publicity by getting a famous artist to design a one-of-a-kind paint job. Braniff presented the idea to Sandy and offered him a $100,000 fee. "It might be fun," Sandy replied. "I'll see what I can come up with." Braniff sent eight scale models, each six feet long, to Saché in December 1972, and Sandy painted them by hand with his characteristic forms and colors. Once the final design was selected, Braniff engineers traced Calder's pattern onto graph paper, enlarged the graph twenty-five times, then transferred the design to an actual DC-8 passenger jet. In October of the next year Sandy flew to Dallas to supervise the paint job. Although the large elements of his design were spray-painted by professional workers, Sandy himself hand-painted some of the thirty-three smaller figures.

"Flying Colors," as the completed airplane was called, looked a great deal like a 157-foot-long, flying Calder gouache, covered with Sandy's typical free-form shapes in bright red, blue, yellow, orange, white and black. In a clever publicity move, Braniff omitted its own name on the outside of the aircraft and, instead, featured Calder's giant yellow signature, thirteen feet long, stenciled prominently next to the door. The plane joined Braniff's fleet in November, 1973, flying between North and South America. The colorful plane was so jaunty and festive in ap-

pearance that, when it touched down at an airport, it almost seemed as though a carnival had come to town.

"Flying Colors" made its first trip to Europe in May 1975, and was displayed for a few days at the Paris Air Show at Le Bourget Airport. Braniff's publicity department, now trying to entice European travelers to the Americas, coaxed Sandy into visiting the air show and painting a couple of new designs on the plane. Sandy agreed, and he and Louisa left Saché for a few

Calder designed this invitation in 1975, inviting friends and acquaintances to join him at Le Bourget Airport in Paris for a two-hour luncheon flight aboard *Flying Colors.*

days in Paris. He was frowning fiercely when he showed up at the airport, possibly because so few people were there to greet him. Wasting no time at all, he picked up a brush and began painting new designs on two of the engine nacelles. His movements were stiff and slow, obviously requiring enormous concentration and effort. Only a few photographers attempted to record the event. Those who requested Sandy to face in a certain direction or hold a particular pose soon realized that he was slowly turning his back on them. For an artist who had always been extremely gifted at self-promotion, Sandy displayed an ambivalent attitude toward public relations during his later years. Often, he agreed to publicize some event, then did so in a surly manner.

In the fall of 1974, Sandy had his annual show —this time of "Crags and Critters"—at the Perls Galleries in New York. The work showed no diminution of vitality or wit. The black "Crags"

Flying Colors, 1973. DC–8 jet, 157' l. Braniff International.

Sandy's colorful design transformed Braniff's jet into a flying gouache. Later he designed a second plane for Braniff, *Flying Colors of the United States,* celebrating the country's two-hundredth birthday.

are standing mobiles that evoke fanciful, miniature mountains. Like the stabiles, the Crags con-
sist mainly of intersecting planes of sheet metal,
each cut with undulating contours. What distin-
guishes the Crags from Sandy's previous mo-
bile-stabile combinations is that the mobile elements are not fastened to the base. Instead, they
are casually perched in the undulating crooks of
the stabile. The spectators have the option of
physically transferring the movable elements
from one location to another, into any nook or
cranny they choose.

The "Critters" were an even bigger surprise—
lifesize, sheet-metal caricatures of naked human

beings. Most of the black figures are bent in a
few strategic places and stand erect on three
legs. Their heads are onion-shaped and their features have the simplicity of a jack-o'-lantern;
eyes and mouths are completely gouged out,
while a narrow incision, like a squared-off U,
delineates the nose. The Critters are fiercely gro-
tesque and, in a cartoony way, very funny. They
manage to be both menacing and whimsical.

In addition to producing unique works of art,
Sandy designed hundreds of prints and posters
that virtually glutted the market. Every frame
shop, coffee house and student dorm throughout
the United States seemed to feature at least one

Calder poster. Meanwhile, a few hundred miles south of Paris, scores of nimble fingers translated Calder designs, with his permission, into impeccably textured Aubusson tapestries. Since even a skilled weaver would spend nearly a month turning out a single square yard of tapestry, these wall-hangings were necessarily expensive—Sandy's royalty accounting for only a small portion of the high price. It was Louisa's idea to employ entire villages of craftspeople in Nicaragua and Guatemala to weave Sandy's designs in coarse yarn, producing hammocks and mats that could be marketed—for about $2,000 apiece—in wealthier countries.

All these commissions, projects and commercial ploys helped make Sandy an enormously rich man. He built himself a larger, more comfortable house in Saché, and turned the first into a guesthouse. Sandy now owned three homes in France, in addition to the one in Roxbury. But he impressed those close to him as being entirely unaffected by wealth. He still wore the same red shirts, and pursued the same simple lifestyle. "Money hasn't changed him at all," Jean Davidson told a visiting reporter in Saché. "He goes to

Critter with Upraised Arm, 1974. Sculpture: painted steel plate, 78" x 39" x 21". The First National Bank of Chicago.

meetings with accountants, they're talking about hundreds of thousands of dollars, and he falls asleep."

But if money was mentioned in Louisa's presence, she gave it her full attention. She seemed to believe that everyone was taking advantage of Sandy and herself, and was resentful that some of Sandy's early collectors, who had bought his work cheaply, were later able to sell it for large profits.

Since Sandy and his art had become one of Saché's leading tourist attractions, Louisa complained about chronic infringement on the family's privacy. "Now we have people who come and peer in our window," she told a reporter in 1973. Once she even turned away a busload of schoolchildren, accompanied by two nuns.

One day in 1973, Louisa remarked airily, "I sometimes say we were much happier when we didn't have money and were left alone."

Les Masques, 1971. Hand-woven Aubusson tapestry, 5'4" x 8'2". Art Vivant, Inc., New Rochelle, New York.

"You didn't like that either," Sandy retorted.

With advancing age, Sandy began to receive awards and honors with great frequency. Important awards and honors almost inevitably come too late to be genuinely useful to the recipient. Also, universities are reluctant to give an honorary degree unless the recipient agrees to show up in person to receive it. Sandy was often torn between his desire to have such awards, and the nuisance of making a personal appearance. His pride usually won out, however, so he made official visits to the University of Hartford, Harvard University and Stevens Institute, which conferred upon him honorary doctorates in fine arts, humanities and engineering, respectively.

Sandy received almost daily invitations to deliver talks or lectures somewhere in the world, and he consistently rejected such requests. As he once said, many years earlier, "One of the problems confronting me is to get enough free time to *work*, and not to go around talking about it."

In addition, there were the retrospective exhibitions that made demands on his time. In 1969 he had major retrospectives at the Fondation Maeght in France and at the Museum of Modern Art in New York. It seemed there was scarcely a moment when a retrospective show of Sandy's work was *not* on display in a museum or gallery somewhere in the western world. Many of the museums and galleries asked for Sandy's cooperation in locating works and providing background information on them.

"We'll never get out of these retrospectives," Sandy said.

The most ambitious retrospective, titled "Calder's Universe," opened at the Whitney Museum in New York in October 1976. It surveyed fifty years of Sandy's career, and contained some two hundred works—including toys, the circus, drawings, works on paper, paintings, tapestries and rugs, household objects, jewelry and, of course, sculpture. The exhibition was organized by Jean Lipman, an art editor and longtime friend of Sandy's, as well as one of his most ardent collectors.

Sandy participated in the preparation of the show and lent many works from his own collection. A few weeks before the show was due to open, he arrived in New York to help install it. Sandy and Louisa intended to stay in the United States for six weeks and, in order to be close to the Whitney Museum, they moved into their daughter Mary's house in downtown Manhattan. Sandy became a familiar sight at the Whitney. He helped set up the circus inside a large display case. As other works were being put into position, he gave instructions on how they should be adjusted or, in some cases, fixed.

Green Ball, 1971. Hand-woven Aubusson tapestry, 6′7″ x 4′6½″. Collection Shirley Polykoff, New York.

Still another adaptation of two of Calder's favored motifs—spheres floating in space and a trained seal balancing a ball.

When he discovered that a mobile from the Museum of Modern Art was bent, he took a pair of pliers and repaired it. Even after the show opened, he arrived one day with a can of paint and a brush and proceeded to touch up a mobile. Museum-goers were delighted to witness this unscheduled event.

Sandy was the guest of honor at an exclusive dinner held at the Whitney Museum prior to the public opening of the show. Some sixty people were invited, including artists Georgia O'Keeffe and Louise Nevelson, architects Marcel Breuer and Philip Johnson, composers Virgil Thomson and John Cage, and authors Arthur Miller and Robert Penn Warren. Sandy and Louisa appeared pleased.

But their mood was far from placid when they showed up for the museum's press preview. Sandy was dressed in his standard outfit—red-flannel shirt, baggy beige pants—but had added a brown tweed jacket and a black-and-yellow tie in an attempt to appear more formal. Louisa wore a loose-fitting dress that resembled a striped tent, embellished with a chunky piece of Sandy's jewelry—a spiraling metal pin. She and Sandy impatiently suffered the attention of newspeople. Sandy ignored many questions and simply walked away from some reporters. To a journalist who asked Louisa when Sandy had made her pin, she haughtily replied, "I don't keep track of such things." When another journalist asked Sandy how he started making his jewelry, Sandy said gruffly, "With a hammer." Both Calders were so uncooperative with the press that one might have wondered why they even bothered to attend the press preview. Amazingly, their rudeness was ignored by most journalists, who continued to perpetuate Sandy's former image as a kind of jovial Santa Claus, overlooking the fact that he was now old, infirm and crusty.

The art critics, by and large, raved over the show, outdoing each other in marveling at Sandy's wit, charm and cleverness. This was nothing new. Writers usually referred to Calder's work in terms of "fun and games," "toys," and "humor." In fact, reviewers seldom were inclined to treat Sandy's art with much seriousness at all. They generally were content to remark that Sandy enlivened abstract art with a sense of humor—an observation that James Johnson Sweeney had made back in the 1940s. But now critics were more willing to concede that Sandy was a major artist. Emily Genauer, for instance, declared that "underneath all the fun and games is one of the most innovative sculptural minds of the twentieth century."

It didn't much matter what any of the critics said, because Sandy had been a popular figure for so long that his Whitney retrospective was bound to be an enormous success. Expectedly, the public turned up in record numbers, standing in line—sometimes for hours—outside the museum, patiently awaiting the "fun and games" inside. Almost every New York newspaper and magazine contributed to the show's popularity by printing photographs of Sandy and articles on his art. His mobiles even appeared on television during the evening news. Art galleries and bookstores along Madison Avenue featured Calder originals or reproductions in window displays, helping to create the impression that the entire city had turned itself into a Calder celebration.

Then, one morning, Sandy's life abruptly came to an end. On Thursday, November 11, 1976, while staying at Mary's house, he suffered a heart attack and died.

Sandy could not have timed his exit any better. He died at the peak of his fame, at a time when he was beloved by more people than ever and was still in good command of his creative powers. He had lived long enough to enjoy numerous retrospectives and to receive considerable acclaim and many accolades. At the time of his death, he was very much on the public's mind, and a generous sampling of his work was on view at the Whitney. Sandy's death was front-page news, and his fellow artists and art-world dignitaries hastened to compose tributes to him. One of the most appreciative came from President Gerald Ford, who declared, "Art has lost a genius and the United States has lost a great American who has contributed much to the civilization of the twentieth century." Once the Whitney retrospective turned into a memorial show, attendance multiplied. After closing in New York in February 1977, the exhibition traveled to museums in Atlanta, Minneapolis and Dallas. The show was thronged with spectators throughout its long run.

A few weeks after Sandy died, a memorial service was held amid his show at the Whitney Museum. About three hundred people crowded into the fourth-floor galleries to look once more at Calder's art and to honor his memory. Of the several eulogies that were delivered, the most touching was James Johnson Sweeney's: "We will miss his dancing and his gruff, sleepy-bear character, as well as his eternal red shirt so symbolic of his personal warmth; but the sense of rhythm, the sense of fun and the capacity for enjoyment, which were essential elements of his life as well as his art, will remain always for us who knew him."

Since Calder's prolific art production had finally come to a halt, the value of his existing works increased dramatically. According to Klaus Perls, the artist's dealer for twenty-two years, Calder didn't earn substantial sums of money before the 1960s. "I remember telling him that we had to get him more money so he could work freely," Perls said. Calder had been skeptical that his mobiles would sell for thousands of dollars, but they did, and Calder's prices continued to rise during the 1960s and '70s.

In April 1978, Louisa designated another New York gallery, M. Knoedler & Company, to be the exclusive, worldwide agent for the Calder estate (valued at between $15 and $25 million). Knoedler estimated there were several hundred pieces of sculpture in the estate; the gallery evaluated the smallest at $15,000 each, the largest at $500,000 each. Knoedler gave Louisa and her family a three-year contract, guaranteeing them $1.5 million and promising to raise Calder's prices still higher.

Klaus Perls was understandably disappointed when he learned he would not be representing the Calder estate. "I'm not really very good at dealing with lawyers and families," he said. "Dealing with Calder, however, was a delight."

At various stages in his life, Calder seemed as aimless and eccentric as the disks on his mobiles,

allowing himself to be swayed and influenced this way and that. As a young American in Paris, he was extremely fortunate to meet with and learn from such important artists as Mondrian, Arp, Miró and Duchamp. Calder was smart enough to recognize some of the most vital, original art of his era, and skillful enough to synthesize the ideas and forms of others into a highly individual type of work that won enormous favor with the public.

In person, Calder was a natural entertainer. In his various guises—circus ringmaster, universe inventor, dancing bear, Yankee tinkerer—he contributed considerable merriment to his world, lifting the spirits of people wherever he went. His playfulness and mechanical ingenuity endeared him to his contemporaries. Happily, these qualities live on in his art, spreading joy year after year.

Sandy and his stabiles outside the Saché studio in 1966.

CHRONOLOGY

1898 Alexander Calder is born in Lawnton, Pennsylvania, on July 22.

1902 He poses for "The Man Cub," a sculpture made by his father, Alexander Stirling Calder.

1905–09 Because of Stirling Calder's poor health, the family moves to Oracle, Arizona, and then on to Pasadena, California.

1910–12 The Calders move to New York, settling first in Croton-on-Hudson, then in Spuyten Duyvil.

1912 Stirling Calder is appointed acting chief of sculpture for the Panama-Pacific Exposition to be held in San Francisco in 1915.

1913–15 The Calders resettle in California; first in San Francisco, and later in Berkeley.

1915 The Calders move to New York City.
Alexander enrolls at Stevens Institute of Technology, in Hoboken, New Jersey.

1916 Stirling Calder is elected to the National Institute of Arts and Letters.

1918 Stirling Calder sculpts a statue of George Washington for the western pier of the Washington Square Arch, New York City.

1919 Alexander Calder graduates from Stevens Institute with a degree in mechanical engineering.

1919–22 Calder moves through a variety of jobs in New Jersey, New York, Missouri, Ohio and West Virginia.

1922 Calder begins drawing lessons in New York City.
In June he takes a job on boat going to San Francisco. He visits his sister in Washington, then works in logging camps on the West Coast.

1923 Alexander Milne Calder, Alexander's grandfather, dies in June.
Calder enters the Art Students League, New York, in the fall, and studies there until 1926.

1924 Calder begins to find occasional work as a free-lance artist.

1925–26 Calder publishes humorous, half-page drawings in *The National Police Gazette*.

1926 Calder publishes *Animal Sketching*.
He has an exhibition of oil paintings at the Artists' Gallery, New York City.
In June he sails to England on a freighter; continues to Paris.
He studies at the Académie de la Grande Chaumière, Paris.
In the fall he makes a free round-trip sailing to New York and back on a Holland-America Line ship, in exchange for drawings of shipboard life to be used in advertisements.

He takes a studio at 22, rue Daguerre, Paris.

He begins a miniature circus, making wooden and wire animals.

He produces toys and animated wire sculpture.

1927   Calder presents his first circus performances at his studio.

In the fall he returns to the United States; he visits Oshkosh, Wisconsin, to negotiate manufacture of "action toys."

1928   An exhibition of Calder's wire sculpture is held at the Weyhe Gallery, New York City, in February.

In November he returns to Paris and takes a ground-floor studio at 7, rue Cels.

He meets Jules Pascin.

1929   An exhibition of Calder's wire portraits and wood sculpture is held at Galerie Billiet, Paris, in January.

"Romulus and Remus" and "Spring" are shown at Salon des Indépendants, Paris.

An exhibition of Calder's wood sculpture is held at Weyhe Gallery, New York.

Calder meets Joan Miró.

Calder goes to Berlin to mount a sculpture exhibition at the Neumann und Nierendorf Gallery.

Calder returns to the United States by ship,

and meets Louisa James, his future wife, in June.

Calder presents a circus performance in New York.

An exhibition of his wood sculpture, paintings, toys and jewelry is held at the Fifty-sixth Street Galleries, New York.

1930   Calder returns to Paris by way of Barcelona in March and takes a studio at 7, Villa Brune.

Calder presents circus performances at his Villa Brune studio during the summer.

Louisa comes to Paris in the summer.

Calder experiments with abstract art as a result of a fall visit to Piet Mondrian's studio.

Calder joins Abstraction-Création, a group of abstract artists.

Calder returns to the United States in December and his work is included in a show of contemporary American art at the Museum of Modern Art, New York.

1931   Calder marries Louisa James in Concord, Massachusetts, on January 17.

The Calders return to the Paris apartment at 7, Villa Brune.

Calder illustrates the book, *Fables of Aesop*.

An exhibition of abstract wire constructions and wire portraits is held at Galerie Percier, Paris, in April. Fernand Léger writes the preface to the catalog.

The Calders rent a house at 14, rue de la Colonie, Paris.

The Calders vacation in Majorca in the summer.

Stirling Calder's statue of Leif Ericsson is installed in Reykjavik, Iceland.

1932   Calder meets Marcel Duchamp.

The first exhibition of mobiles—a word suggested by Duchamp—is held in February, at Galerie Vignon, Paris. Arp coins the word stabiles for motionless sculpture.

The Calders return to the United States in May.

An exhibition of mobiles is held at the Julien Levy Gallery, New York, in May.

The Calders return to Paris, in the fall, by way of Spain where they visit Miró and present a circus performance in Montroig.

1933   Calder presents circus performances in Madrid and Barcelona in February.

Calder participates in a spring, group show (with Arp, Hélion, Miró, Pevsner and Seligmann) at Galerie Pierre, Paris.

An exhibit, "recent work," is held at the Pierre Colle Galerie, Paris, in May.

The Calders return to the United States in June.

The Calders buy a farmhouse in Roxbury, Connecticut, in the summer.

1934   The first of several one-man exhibitions of Calder's work is held at the Pierre Matisse Gallery, New York, in April.

1935   An exhibition of mobiles is held in January, in Chicago.

The Calders' daughter Sandra is born on April 20.

Calder designs the setting for a Martha Graham ballet.

1936   Calder designs scenery for a production of Erik Satie's *Socrate,* performed in Hartford, Connecticut.

1937   The Calders go to France in May.

Calder makes "Mercury Fountain" for the Spanish Pavilion at the Paris Exposition.

The Calders vacation in Varengeville, France, in the summer.

A December exhibition of mobiles, stabiles and jewelry is held at the Mayor Gallery in London. The Calders spend the winter in England.

1938   The Calders return to the United States in the spring and divide their time between the Roxbury home and a New York apartment.

The first comprehensive museum exhibition is held in November, at the George Walter

Vincent Smith Art Museum, Springfield, Massachusetts.

Calder builds a new studio at Roxbury.

1939   The Calders' daughter Mary is born on May 25.

1940   An exhibition of jewelry is held at the Willard Gallery, New York.

1941   The second exhibition of jewelry is held at the Willard Gallery.

1942   Calder's mobiles and stabiles are exhibited in a two-man show (with Paul Klee's paintings) at the Cincinnati Art Museum in April.

Calder's work is included in a group show, "First Papers of Surrealism," in New York in October.

Calder studies civilian camouflage and assists in occupational therapy training.

1943   Calder makes a series of wire-and-wood constructions, called Constellations.

A fire destroys part of the Roxbury house in the fall.

A Calder retrospective exhibition is held in November at the Museum of Modern Art, New York.

1944   Calder illustrates *Three Young Rats*, a book of old English rhymes.

1945   Stirling Calder dies at age seventy-four in New York, in January.

The French philosopher Jean-Paul Sartre visits Calder at Roxbury.

1946   Calder flies to Paris in June to arrange a show.

An exhibition of mobiles is held in October, at Galerie Louis Carré, Paris.

1947   Calder participates in a summer, two-man exhibition (with Léger) at Stedelijk Museum in Amsterdam and the Kunsthalle in Bern.

Miró visits the Calders in Roxbury.

1948   The Calders travel to Brazil in the summer for a September exhibition in Rio de Janeiro and São Paulo.

1949   Calder makes "International Mobile," his largest to date—20' x 20'.

1950   The Calders visit Paris in the spring.

An exhibition of mobiles and stabiles is held at Galerie Maeght, Paris, in June.

The Calders visit Finland and Sweden in August.

The Calders return to Roxbury in September.

A Calder retrospective exhibition is held at Massachusetts Institute of Technology, Cambridge, Massachusetts, in December.

1951   Calder exhibitions are held in London, Vienna and Houston.

1952 Calder represents the United States in June at the Venice Biennale; he wins the sculpture prize.

Calder travels in West Germany in September.

Calder designs an acoustic ceiling for an auditorium in University City, Caracas, Venezuela.

1953 The Calders sail to France in June, and they acquire a house in Saché.

Calder starts producing gouaches in quantity.

1954 The Calders travel to Lebanon in January, where Sandy designs a mobile for an airline office in Beirut.

Louisa and Mary return to the United States; Calder follows about a month later.

An exhibition of standing mobiles is held in October at Galerie Maeght, Paris.

1955 Calder and Louisa travel to India in January.

A spring Calder retrospective exhibition is held at Curt Valentin Gallery, New York.

Calder flies to Caracas in August to arrange an exhibition at the Museo de Bellas Artes.

Sandra Calder marries Jean Davidson in Saché, France, on October 28.

1956 The Calders' first grandchild, Shawn Davidson, is born in Tours, France, in October.

Calder has the first of many exhibitions at Perls Galleries, New York.

1957 The Calders visit friends in Brittany and buy a deteriorated house facing the English Channel.

1958 Calder designs a large motorized mobile, "The Whirling Ear," for the World's Fair at Brussels.

Calder designs a large standing mobile, "The Spiral," for the UNESCO building in Paris.

Calder oversees the installation of a forty-five-foot-long mobile, ".125," at Kennedy Airport, New York.

Calder wins a prize at the Carnegie International Exhibition, Pittsburgh.

1959 An exhibition of large stabiles is held in February at Galerie Maeght, Paris.

A Calder exhibition is held at Museu de Arte Moderna, Rio de Janeiro, in September.

1960 Calder and Louisa fly to Rio de Janeiro in February to attend the carnival.

Nanette Lederer Calder, Calder's mother, dies at age ninety-three in New Milford, Connecticut, on March 12.

1961   Mary Calder marries Howard Rower on April 4.

1962   Calder builds a new studio at Saché.

Calder retrospective exhibition is held at the Tate Gallery, London, in July.

Calder designs a fifty-nine-foot-high stabile, "Teodelapio," for Spoleto, Italy.

1964   A huge Calder retrospective exhibition in November fills the entire Guggenheim Museum, New York; the show later travels in reduced form to Milwaukee, St. Louis, Des Moines and Ottawa.

1965   A Calder retrospective exhibition is held in July at the Musée National d'Art Moderne, Paris.

Calder oversees the installation of forty-foot-high stabile, "The Big Sail," at Massachusetts Institute of Technology, Cambridge, Massachusetts, in the fall.

1966   Calder publishes his autobiography.

Calder gives eighteen works to the Museum of Modern Art, New York.

1967   An exhibition of Calder's gifts is held at the Museum of Modern Art, New York.

Calder oversees the installation of a seventy-foot-high stabile, "Man," at Expo '67, Montreal, in April.

1968   "Work in Progress," a nineteen-minute theater piece, is performed in Rome.

Calder designs an eighty-foot-high stabile, "Red Sun," for Aztec Stadium, Mexico City.

1969   A Calder retrospective exhibition is held in April at Fondation Maeght in Saint-Paul-de-Vence, France.

The dedication of large stabile, "La Grande Vitesse," takes place in Grand Rapids, Michigan, in June.

"A Salute to Alexander Calder," an exhibition at New York's Museum of Modern Art, is held in December.

1970   The Calders move into a new house in Saché, and keep the former one as a guesthouse.

1971   An exhibition of "animobiles" and gouaches is held at Perls Galleries, New York, in October.

1972   A retrospective exhibition of "Calder's Circus" is held at the Whitney Museum of American Art, New York, in April.

Calder designs a small bronze stabile, called the "Sandy," which is awarded annually, by the Art Dealers Association of America, Inc.

1973   "Stegosaurus," a fifty-foot-high stabile, is erected next to city hall in Hartford, Connecticut.

"Flying Colors," a DC-8 passenger jet,

spray-painted with Calder designs, begins flights between North and South America in November.

1974 A Calder Festival takes place in Chicago in October to celebrate the dedication of two important works: "Flamingo," a fifty-three-foot-high stabile commissioned by the United States General Services Administration for Federal Center Plaza, and "Universe," a motorized mural for the Sears Tower.

A Calder retrospective exhibition is held in October at the Museum of Contemporary Art in Chicago.

The "Crags and Critters" exhibition is held at Perls Galleries, New York, in October.

1975 Calder-designed Aubusson tapestries are exhibited at Wesleyan University in Connecticut in January.

Calder-designed hammocks and floor mats, handwoven by Central American Indians, are displayed in New York in March.

The Calders visit Israel in April, where Calder agrees to design a stabile for Jerusalem. The stabile is completed and installed posthumously.

"Flying Colors" is displayed at the Paris Air Show in May; Calder visits Le Bourget Airport to hand-paint new designs on two of the plane's engine covers. Models for "Flying Colors" are exhibited at Galerie Maeght in Paris.

A Calder retrospective exhibition opens in May at Haus der Kunst in Munich; the show later travels to the Kunsthaus in Zurich.

A Calder-designed BMW racing car competes at Le Mans in France in June.

"Flying Colors of the United States," another Braniff airplane with Calder designs, is dedicated in Washington, D.C., in November.

1976 A five-day Calder celebration in October in Philadelphia includes: the dedication of a monumental mobile, "White Cascade," at the Federal Reserve Bank; the unveiling of a mural at the Philadelphia College of Art; and the re-creation of the 1936 stage sets for a new production of Satie's *Socrate* by the Philadelphia Composers' Forum.

"Calder's Universe," a major retrospective, opens in October and draws record attendance at the Whitney Museum of American Art in New York. The show later toured Atlanta, Minneapolis and Dallas.

Alexander Calder dies at age seventy-eight in New York City, on November 11.

SELECTED BIBLIOGRAPHY

BY CALDER

Alexander Calder Papers. Archives of American Art. Washington, D.C.: Smithsonian Institution. Approximately 2,000 documents—including letters, photographs, exhibition announcements, magazine and newspaper clippings, address books and passport—available on microfilm. Duplicate microfilm rolls are in other Archives offices in Boston, Detroit, New York and San Francisco.

Calder, Alexander. *Calder: An Autobiography with Pictures.* New York: Pantheon Books, 1966.

ILLUSTRATED BY CALDER

Calder, Alexander. *Animal Sketching.* Text by Charles Liedl; illustrations by Calder. Pelham, New York: Bridgman Publishers, Inc., 1926. Reprint, New York: Sterling Publishing Co., Inc., 1972.

Coleridge, Samuel. *The Rime of the Ancient Mariner.* Essay by Robert Penn Warren; drawings by Calder. New York: Reynal and Hitchcock, 1946.

Fables of Aesop/According to Sir Roger L'Estrange. Drawings by Calder. Paris: Harrison of Paris, 1931. Paperback reprint, New York: Dover Publications, Inc., 1967.

La Fontaine, Jean de. *Selected Fables.* Translated by Eunice Clark; drawings by Calder. New York: George Braziller, Inc., 1948. Paperback reprint, New York: Dover Publications, Inc., 1968.

Three Young Rats and Other Rhymes. Edited, and with an introduction by James Johnson Sweeney; drawings by Calder. New York: Curt Valentin, 1944. Reprint, New York: Museum of Modern Art, 1946.

Wilbur, Richard, ed. *A Bestiary.* Illustrated by Calder. New York: Pantheon Books, 1955.

ABOUT CALDER

BOOKS

Arnason, H.H. and Guerrero, Pedro E. *Calder*. Princeton, N.J.: Van Nostrand, 1966. Text by Arnason; photographs by Guerrero.

Hayes, Margaret Calder. *Three Alexander Calders/A Family Memoir*. Middlebury, Vt.: Paul S. Eriksson, 1977.

Homage to Alexander Calder. G. di San Lazzaro, ed. Special issue of *XXe siècle* (Paris). New York: Tudor Publishing Co., 1972. Contains essays (in English) by numerous contributors.

Kuh, Katharine. *The Artist's Voice/Talks with Seventeen Artists*. New York and Evanston: Harper & Row, 1960. Calder interview, pp. 38–51.

Lipman, Jean. *Calder's Universe*. New York: Viking Press, in cooperation with the Whitney Museum of American Art, 1976.

Lipman, Jean, with Nancy Foote, eds. *Calder's Circus*. New York: E.P. Dutton & Co., Inc., in association with the Whitney Museum of American Art, 1972.

Mancewicz, Bernice Winslow. *Alexander Calder/A Pictorial Essay*. Grand Rapids, Michigan: William B. Eerdmans, 1969.

Mulas, Ugo and Arnason, H.H. *Calder*. New York: Viking Press, 1971. Photographs by Mulas; introduction by Arnason, with comments by Calder.

Rodman, Selden. *Conversations with Artists*. New York: Devin-Adair Co., 1957. Paperback reprint, New York: Capricorn Books, 1961. Calder interview, pp. 136–42.

MAGAZINE ARTICLES *(listed chronologically)*

Hellman, Geoffrey T. "Everything Is Mobile." *The New Yorker*, Oct. 4, 1941, pp. 25–30, 33.

Hellman, Geoffrey T. "Calder Revisited." *The New Yorker*, Oct. 22, 1960, pp. 163–64, 167ff.

Davidson, Jean. "Four Calders." *Art in America*, Vol. 50, no. 4 (Winter 1962), pp. 68–73.

Gray, Francine du Plessix. "At the Calders'." *House & Garden,* Dec. 1963, pp. 155–59, 189.

Andersen, Wayne V. "Calder at the Guggenheim." *Artforum,* Vol. 3, no. 6 (March 1965), pp. 37–41.

Russell, John. "Alexander Calder in Saché." *Vogue,* July 1967, pp. 110–15, 119, 121, 130.

"Calder On-stage." *Newsweek,* March 25, 1968, p. 100.

Osborn, Robert. "Calder's International Monuments." *Art in America,* Vol. 57, no. 2 (March–April 1969), pp. 32–49.

Alloway, Lawrence. "Art." *The Nation,* April 24, 1972, pp. 541–42.

Morgan, Ted. "A Visit to Calder Kingdom." *The New York Times Magazine,* July 8, 1973, pp. 10–11, 29 ff.

Kramer, Hilton. "Toys, Trivets and Serving Trays." *The New York Times Magazine,* Oct. 17, 1976, pp. 70–71, 73–76.

Russell, John. "Alexander Calder, Leading U.S. Artist, Dies." *The New York Times,* Nov. 12, 1976, pp. A1, D14.

Halasz, Piri. "America's Own Version of Matisse and/or Picasso—'Sandy' Calder." *Smithsonian,* Vol. 7, no. 9 (December 1976), pp. 74–81.

Goldin, Amy. "Alexander Calder, 1898–1976." *Art in America,* Vol. 65, no. 2 (March–April 1977), pp. 70–73.

EXHIBITION CATALOGS *(listed chronologically)*

The Museum of Modern Art, New York. Sept. 29, 1943–Jan. 16, 1944. *Alexander Calder.* Text by James Johnson Sweeney. Revised edition, 1951.

The Solomon R. Guggenheim Museum, New York. Nov. 1964–Jan. 1965. *Alexander Calder/A Retrospective Exhibition.* Introduction by Thomas M. Messer.

The Museum of Fine Arts, Houston. Nov. 24–Dec. 13, 1964. *Alexander Calder/ Circus Drawings, Wire Sculpture and Toys.* Introduction by James Johnson Sweeney.

Musée National d'Art Moderne, Paris. July–Oct. 1965. *Calder.* Preface by Jean Cassou.

Fondation Maeght, Saint-Paul, France. April 2–May 31, 1969. *Calder,* Texts (in French) by several contributors.

The Museum of Modern Art, New York. Dec. 22, 1969–Feb. 15, 1970. *A Salute to Alexander Calder.* Introductory essay by Bernice Rose.

Museum of Contemporary Art, Chicago. Oct. 26–Dec. 8, 1974. *Alexander Calder/A Retrospective Exhibition/Work from 1925 to 1974.* Essay by Albert E. Elsen; forward by Stephen Prokopoff.

Haus der Kunst, Munich. May 10–July 13, 1975. *Calder.* Essay (in German) by Maurice Besset.

BOOKS ON TWENTIETH-CENTURY AMERICAN ART

Burnham, Jack. *Beyond Modern Sculpture: The Effects of Science and Technology on the Sculpture of this Century.* New York: George Braziller, Inc., 1968.

Craven, Wayne. *Sculpture in America.* New York: Thomas Y. Crowell Co., 1968.

Goldwater, Robert. *What Is Modern Sculpture?* New York: The Museum of Modern Art, 1969; distributed by New York Graphic Society, Ltd., Greenwich, Connecticut.

Hunter, Sam. *American Art of the 20th Century.* New York: Harry N. Abrams, Inc., 1972.

Krauss, Rosalind E. *Passages in Modern Sculpture.* New York: Viking Press, 1977.

Rose, Barbara. *American Art Since 1900.* New York: Praeger Publishers, Inc., 1975.

The Britannica Encyclopedia of American Art. Chicago: Encyclopedia Britannica Educational Corp., 1973; distributed by Simon and Schuster, New York.

200 Years of American Sculpture. David R. Godine, Publisher, in association with the Whitney Museum of American Art, 1976.

INDEX

Numbers in bold face refer to illustrations.

ABOUT THE AUTHOR

David Bourdon is a widely published art writer noted for his expertise in twentieth-century art. A former editor of *Life* and *Smithsonian* magazines, he contributes articles to numerous magazines and writes a regular column for *Vogue.* He is the author of *Christo,* a major book on the contemporary sculptor, and consulting editor on *Christo: Running Fence.* Mr. Bourdon lives in New York where he keeps a close watch on the art scene.